LIVING
on
Our HEADS

LIVING
on
Our HEADS

ROD PARSLEY

FRONT LINE

Most STRANG COMMUNICATIONS BOOK GROUP products are available at special quantity discounts for bulk purchase for sales promotions, premiums, fund-raising, and educational needs. For details, write Strang Communications Book Group, 600 Rinehart Road, Lake Mary, Florida 32746, or telephone (407) 333-0600.

LIVING ON OUR HEADS by Rod Parsley
Published by FrontLine
A Strang Company
600 Rinehart Road
Lake Mary, Florida 32746
www.strangbookgroup.com

Unless otherwise noted, all Scripture quotations are from the New American Standard Bible. Copyright © 1960, 1962, 1963, 1968, 1971, 1972, 1973, 1975, 1977, 1995 by the Lockman Foundation. Used by permission. (www.Lockman.org)

Scripture quotations marked NKJV are from the New King James Version of the Bible. Copyright © 1979, 1980, 1982 by Thomas Nelson, Inc., publishers. Used by permission.

Scripture quotations marked NIV are from the Holy Bible, New International Version. Copyright © 1973, 1978, 1984, International Bible Society. Used by permission.

Cover photograph by Sarah Smith of Kent Smith Photography
Cover design by Justin Evans
Design Director: Bill Johnson

Library of Congress Cataloging-in-Publication Data
Parsley, Rod.
  Living on our heads / Rod Parsley. -- 1st ed.
      p. cm.
  Includes bibliographical references and index.
  ISBN 978-1-61638-188-2
  1. Christianity and culture--United States. 2. United States--Social conditions--21st century. 3. United States--History--21st century. I. Title.
  BR517.P37 2010
  261.0973--dc22
                                        2010020903
First Edition

10 11 12 13 14 — 9 8 7 6 5 4 3 2 1
Printed in the United States of America

CONTENTS

Part 3
Adults Are Children...
Children Are Adults

Part 4
Headstands and Heads Up

A CULTURE OF "CONTRARIES"

A NATIVE AMERICAN RIDES proudly and defiantly into the village—seated backward on his horse. His puzzled, long-lost stepbrother looks on. "Younger Bear" climbs down from his horse, greets his relative by saying "Good-bye!" and proceeds to bathe by throwing handfuls of dirt all over himself. He finishes by walking down to the river to dry off with water.

You may recognize this ridiculous scene from the 1970 Dustin Hoffman movie *Little Big Man*. In it, Hoffman's character is told that Younger Bear has become a "Contrary"—a person with a mental disorder that causes him to approach everything precisely backward.

Unfortunately, it's not all that uncommon. It can happen to the most unlikely people at the most inconvenient times. If it happens to afflict someone in a position of great responsibility during a time of crisis, the results can be disastrous.

For instance, pilots have to be instrument rated in order to fly during conditions when they are unable to see the ground. If they're flying through clouds or at night, they have to depend completely on what their instruments tell them rather than relying on information sent to the command center of their brain through their senses. It's quite a discipline, and if they fail, they may fall prey to a condition popularly known as vertigo, which affects their equilibrium and causes them to think down is up and up is down. As you can imagine, if uncorrected, their error will lead to terrible tragedy and loss.

I've found myself thinking about poor, confused Younger Bear often in the decade-and-change since our calendars rolled over to 2000 amid the nail-biting, frenzied days of Y2K. On more occasions than I care to count,

I've witnessed acts and statements of breathtaking upside-down-itude and stunning backward-ity. A recent body wash commercial featured a man riding a horse backward. It was amusing because it was absurd—but some people fail to see the humor in it because for them it's normal. After all, sad to say, he's just expressing his individuality and creativity; and yes, cries PETA (People for the Ethical Treatment of Animals), it's perfect, because we wouldn't want the horse to develop an inferiority complex thinking only the rider knows where they should go!

Why does it seem so many people consistently get it wrong? Perhaps this example will help explain.

When I visited Honolulu for the first time, I saw the beautiful waves coming into the beach from the top of a mountain, and I wanted to go experience the thrill of the surf in Hawaii. As I drove down the mountain, I couldn't help but notice that the waves seemed larger and larger, but that didn't deter my naivety or my enthusiasm. I pulled my little rented vehicle into the parking area and ran out into those glorious whitecaps.

Before I got very far, one of those waves that looked so beautiful from a distance picked me up and body-slammed me to the ocean floor. I felt like I was in a washing machine set on the spin cycle. I was rolled across the bottom like a piece of driftwood, with water and sand shooting into...well, you understand. I literally couldn't tell which end was up. At one point the top of my head was parallel with the sandy ocean floor and my feet were saluting the sky. I was...in a word...upside down! I was about to despair of life when that wave, much like Jonah's whale, deposited my scratched and bruised body and ego with great disdain back on the exquisite beach, where I was all too happy to spend the rest of my day with my feet solidly on the ground.

That was more than enough disorientation for me, but it seems that many today enjoy walking on their heads supported only by the unpredictable waves of cultural, political, and spiritual correctness.

When I saw Senate Majority Leader Harry Reid standing in the hallowed well of the Senate proclaiming that the war in Iraq was lost,[1] despite overwhelming evidence that the Bush-Petraeus troop surge was working, I saw a man riding his horse backward—and doing so with the posture and pomp of Stonewall Jackson inspecting the troops. I hadn't seen a leader that eager to declare defeat since an Iraqi sergeant and his men surrendered to an unmanned drone during the first Gulf War.

I watched college campus "intellectuals" wail and rend their clothing as they accused George W. Bush of endangering their free-speech rights. Then I watched Yale students shout down an invited speaker who represented the Minutemen (a pro-border security group), even storming the podium to physically drive the speaker from the stage. Why? Because they didn't like his message. To me, it was as insane as a group of people rolling in dirt while bragging about their hygiene.

And when I see pampered, privileged Hollywood celebrities worshiped like gods while heroic servicemen are criticized and even demonized by fringe groups, I see a culture that has managed to convince itself that up is down and *Good-bye* means *Hello!*

There is no sign of right-side-up-ness when Chris "I felt a thrill run up my leg when Obama spoke"[2] Matthews and his colleagues at MSNBC complain about ideological bias at FOX News. I scratch my head and think, "Well, Mr. Pot, say hello to Mr. Kettle." On the other hand, I shake my head in equal disbelief when conservative clergymen make solemn pronouncements that disasters such as Hurricane Katrina are God's judgment on a city or nation.

Sometimes it seems as though whole segments of our society have become Contraries. And I question if we're becoming "Younger Bear Nation": the obvious is ignored, common sense is disparaged, good is seen as evil, and evil is hailed as good.

As I look around, I see people who favor accommodation for the workplace demands of Muslims but yet, in the next breath, insist that Christians leave their convictions at home. Need a foot bath installed in the break room? No problem! Just don't leave an open Bible on your desk during your lunch break—that is, not if you expect to keep your job. After all, jobs are all too scarce these days, aren't they?

University officials roll out the red carpet to Holocaust-denying thugs but treat a former Harvard president—who dared wonder aloud whether men and women are wired differently—like...well, like a Holocaust-denying thug.[3]

Our culture aggressively markets products and lifestyles to children as though they were adults (consider sexually charged fast-food ads) while marketing to adults as though they were children (desperately in need of more "toys"). More people watch "fake" news shows on television than watch any of the big network newscasts.

Do these examples sound like the makings of an epidemic of upside-down thinking? I believe so.

Of course, these are just the random observations from a country preacher's perspective. Yet lest you think it's just me being an alarmist, I can assure you there is little comfort to be found in the scientific opinion surveys.

For example, one survey for the 2008 election showed that 13 percent of Americans were prepared to cast a vote for a comedian who was pretending to run for president.[4] Meanwhile, psychologists have identified a new compulsion called Celebrity Worship Syndrome (CWS), and one study indicates that 36 percent of Americans may have it.[5] I had an unusual opportunity to see this up close at the Grammy Awards ceremony in 2010. A lady sitting near me was extending her condolences to Lady Gaga for not winning the Album of the Year award. The pop diva pouted like a preschooler and said, "I already won two Grammys anyway." Another poll indicated that more than a third of Americans suspect their own government of being complicit in the horrific attacks of September 11, 2001.[6] (Whether there was a corresponding spike in the sale of tinfoil hats was not reported in the poll.)

In George Orwell's *1984*, you find an entire society brainwashed into accepting absurdities such as:

- War Is Peace
- Freedom Is Slavery
- Ignorance Is Strength[7]

Orwell's novel is just that—a story. However, what we are seeing today is real. To my left, a significant slice of our nation has bought into such bizarre ideas as: "Pop stars are wise." "Al Gore is our savior." "FOX News is the devil." Such beliefs prove once and for all that truth is indeed stranger than fiction.

To be fair, I see another segment on the far edges to my right; this group has become convinced that "Jews are sneaky," "FEMA is a sinister Illuminati plot," and "Katie Couric sleeps hanging upside down from an attic rafter."

Upside-down thinking happens on both sides—and it's nothing new. As I read history, I discover that we are not the first culture to lose track of the general direction of *up* on a large scale.

Take the French Revolution, when a so-called Enlightenment produced bloodthirsty mobs with pitchforks and torches. The hundreds who died daily at the guillotines probably enjoyed all the enlightenment they could bear. For a movement supposedly built on the worship of reason, the French Revolution sure produced a lot of nuttiness—not to mention headless bodies.

Centuries earlier, the Roman Empire prided itself on its wisdom, refinement, and civilization. Eventually, however, the wheels started coming off the chariot of cultural sanity, producing emperors who had all the reasoning power of Charles Manson—but with only half his moral fiber. As for refinement, the general public's idea of a grand day of entertainment consisted of watching people fight, bleed, and die in gladiator games.

The prophet Isaiah knew a raging case of Younger Bear Syndrome when he saw it. Seven hundred years before the birth of Christ, he looked at his neighbors and wrote: "Woe to those who call evil good, and good evil; who substitute darkness for light and light for darkness; who substitute bitter for sweet and sweet for bitter!"[8]

That is as fine a description of upside-down thinking as you'll find. "Woe" is right. And "Whoa!" too. Old Isaiah was doing his best to flag down his fellow citizens who had all piled into a wagon and merrily sent it hurtling toward the nearest cliff.

On the pages that follow I hope to follow Isaiah's example. In order to do that I am going to have to call foolishness what it is.

Wherever nonsense-on-stilts parades itself around our popular culture like an out-of-control Shriner on the Fourth of July, I must point to it with all the indignation that is proper to its outrage.

But I'll do more. Where we've lost our way, I'll direct us to a reliable compass that always points true north. Where we're culturally dizzy and disoriented, I'll point up. Where we're happily careening toward a precipice like Thelma and Louise, I'll wave my arms and shout like the old-school preacher I am.

You see, there's absurdity, and then there's madness—and our culture is descending into a unique form of madness. But it may not be too late. Perhaps I can show us a way out in the next few pages. Come on. Let's see if we can march through the crazy storm of our time to locate some good old-fashioned reality—and with some common sense-ability, stop living on our heads and actually try walking on our feet again.

PART 1

THE BAD GUYS ARE GOOD...
THE GOOD GUYS ARE BAD

OVERVIEW

ONE OF MY most poignant childhood memories, not unlike that of many of my baby-boomer brethren, I'm sure, was Saturday morning with my bowl of Sugar Pops—as they were called before political correctness required a name change to "Corn Pops"—a black-and-white TV complete with three channels, rabbit ears, and my thirty-minute fantasy: I was Tonto, and he was Kimosabe—and he was right and Silver was white! Hi ho! In old westerns like *The Lone Ranger*, identifying the bad guys was easy enough. They were the ones wearing the black Stetsons. More recently, in any *Star Wars* movie, you just had to find the guy whose light saber glowed red. And in almost any other movie or TV drama shot between 1950 and 2000, you only had to be on the lookout for a goatee. Facial hair was always and only worn by the ne'er-do-well—unless, of course, it was a Christmas movie.

The formula was simple: if the writers wanted a character to have an "evil twin," they just glued a Van Dyke on the guy. Presto! Instant sinister alter ego! However, here in the new millennium, knowing who the bad guys are is apparently much more challenging—especially in real life.

One of the most glaring indicators that we are in the midst of a long-term cultural headstand is the widespread inability or refusal to call the clearly wicked *bad* and the obviously heroic *good*. In fact, we have grown way too nuanced and sophisticated for the very concepts of *good* and *evil*.

Witness the mass mockery and involuntary eye-rolling invariably triggered by President George W. Bush's occasional use of the term *evildoers* to describe the people who hope to perpetrate terror attacks on American soil. Mr. Bush's free and unself-conscious use of the term *evil* was Exhibit A in the sophisticated crowd's case that Bush was, at best, a knuckle-dragging Neanderthal and, at worst, a dangerous religious fanatic.

The stubborn insistence on viewing things as either right or wrong was seen as being *so* last century. "It's all a matter of one's perspective," the postmodern thinkers told us.

This twisted, trendy pose was captured perfectly in the saying: "One man's terrorist is another man's freedom fighter." We no longer hold those who commit atrocities responsible for their actions. Instead, we wring our hands and search for "root causes." (Here's a root cause for you: some people are as mean as junkyard dogs.) By the way, I own a couple of those dogs. I had three, but one bit an "upside-down-thinking" blogger and died of food poisoning!

Upside-down-itude and backward-ity is graphically illustrated by an obsession to blame the victims.

"America was attacked because we deserved it," we were told. Even in the raw days immediately following September 11, 2001, such inverted thinking was commonplace. As author Dan Flynn reported: "One confused undergraduate... [said], 'sometimes it is our fault,' while another opined that 'we had it coming.' A professor in New Mexico told his students, 'Anyone who can blow up the Pentagon would get my vote.'"[1]

Of course, none of these valiant contenders for the "Younger Bear Prize for Distinguished Confusion" can hold a burned-out candle to real, live faux-Indian Ward Churchill. You may recall that, as a University of Colorado professor, Churchill made himself the darling of the blame-America-first crowd by writing an essay in which he compared the secretaries and stockbrokers who died in the World Trade Center attacks to officials in Hitler's Nazi party. "Little Eichmanns"[2] he called them. But wait, there's more! Exemplifying the finest and best in head-standing agility, Ward Churchill went on to write:

As to those in the World Trade Center, well, really, let's get a grip here, shall we? True enough, they were civilians of a sort. But innocent? Gimme a break. They formed a technocratic corps at the very heart of America's global financial empire—the "mighty engine of profit" to which the military dimension of U.S. policy has always been enslaved—and they did so both willingly and knowingly.[3]

Yes, ex-Professor Churchill, let's do get a grip here. Please. And while you're working on that, we quasi-soldiers in America's "technocratic corps" will try to stop enslaving the military in pursuit of our global financial empire—or at least cut back some. We're not making any promises, though.

Such is the extreme to which this brand of convoluted thinking can go. But it is not the only example of good guy/bad guy confusion muddying the waters of these shark-infested times. In this first section, I will point to nine more stunning examples of this growing genre.

As you're about to see, a lot of prominent Americans desperately need us to go back to the days of black hats and Van Dykes. Their ability to know a bad guy when they see one has gone spectacularly wrong.

FAWNING OVER THUGS

JUST WHAT IS it about a swaggering dictator on the rise that pop culture icons and Ivy League intellectuals find so irresistible? Why do those who are quickest to speechify about the importance of artistic and intellectual freedom in this country fall all over themselves to hang out with brutal despots in other nations who suppress those very freedoms? How can it be that those who are quickest to get the vapors and swoon when a few grandmothers in flyover country protest filth posing as art are the very ones defending and praising men who kill or imprison anyone who dares to criticize them?

These are questions that defy logical answers. They only make sense if you stand on your head—or earn $100 million a year for looking fabulous.

The latest darling of the elite socialites is Venezuela's dictator-in-the-making, Hugo Chavez. Yet, even before Hugo was a twinkle in Sean Penn's eye, there was Fidel Castro, a cult figure whose office has seen more celebrity visitors than the William Morris Agency.

For decades the Castro dictatorship was artificially propped up by the Soviet Union, which was keenly interested in having a puppet client state on America's doorstep. Cuba was valuable, even though the Soviets' plan to pepper the island with nuclear missile launchers didn't work out as hoped.

Like any Communist dictator worthy of the name, Castro (who was replaced as head of state by brother Raúl in 2008) always crushed opposition, controlled information, owned the press, suppressed dissent, and encouraged a cultlike worship of himself by "the people." Wow—is it just me, or does that sound increasingly like the slippery slope upon which America is currently skiing on its head?

Anyone interested in knowing what it's like to be a person of conscience inside Castro's island paradise should read Armando Valladares's *Against All Hope: A Memoir of Life in Castro's Gulag*. Valladares was a poet who, shortly after Castro's so-called glorious revolution, was jailed in a crackdown on dissidents. He was sent to the gulag for refusing to place on his desk a placard that praised Communism.

Across the next two decades Valladares was subjected to some of the cruelest and most dehumanizing treatments imaginable, yet the Castro regime's tormentors were never able to break his will. As one source states:

> Valladares, unlike many of his fellow political prisoners, survived the forced labor camps. He survived years of solitary confinement. When, in 1963, Valladares was given a blue uniform to wear (the uniform that distinguished common criminals from political prisoners), he refused, electing to go naked until 1983. During 22 years of confinement, Armando Valladares received 13 visits.
>
> Valladares' refusal to participate in any political rehabilitation programs elicited a swift response from the government—46 days without food. His weakened muscles relegated him to a wheelchair for 5 years.[1]

Of course, Valladares is only one of tens of thousands in Cuba who have suffered in the horrific ways dissidents and Christians invariably do under Communist dictators. But that hasn't stopped some of America's most talented and influential people from treating Castro like a shining blend of Santa Claus, Albert Schweitzer, and Obi-Wan Kenobi.

Steven Spielberg visited Cuba in 2002, dining and hanging out with Castro into the wee hours of the morning. In the cigar-smoke tinged afterglow, Spielberg proclaimed his dinner with Castro to be "the eight most important hours of my life."[2]

Is it just me, or does that comment reveal more about all the other hours of Spielberg's life than it does about Castro?

When I heard of filmmaker Michael Moore's attempt to identify the Cuban health care system as the model to which all other nations should aspire, I felt like saying to him and everyone else who acts as though they would like to live in Castro's workers' paradise, "Dude! There's your country!"

After a 1998 meeting with el Presidente, Jack Nicholson declared Castro to be a genius, saying, "We spoke about everything."[3]

Model Naomi Campbell gushed that Castro was "a source of inspiration to the world."[4]

Well, at least we know he inspired Idi Amin, Slobodan Milosevic, Robert Mugabe, and of course his protégé, Hugo Chavez.

"I'm so nervous and flustered because I can't believe I have met him. He said that seeing us in person was very spiritual," Campbell gushed when describing hers and fellow-model Kate Moss's 1999 visit to Cuba.[5]

I'm guessing Castro is not the first fellow to try the old "spiritual connection" line on a couple of supermodels, but at the time, he may have been the first creepy seventy-year-old to actually pull it off.

Joining the gullible parade of Hollywood celebrities who have made the pilgrimage are Woody Harrelson, Oliver Stone, Robert Redford, Sidney Pollack, Danny Glover, Ed Asner, Shirley MacLaine, Alanis Morissette, Spike Lee, Leonardo DiCaprio, and Kevin Costner.

Sadly, none of this is new. Back in the 1930s Joseph Stalin was the toast of the literary and arts crowds from London to Los Angeles. While Stalin was intentionally starving to death an estimated seven to nine million peasants in the Ukraine,[6] he was being toasted at lavish parties by British and American novelists and intellectuals. Even as Stalin routinely rounded up and executed dissidents and his country slipped into poverty, a stream of celebrities visited Moscow and came back declaring they had seen the bright future of mankind.[7]

No, the tendency by some to fawn over thugs is not new. But it has never been so widespread or so dangerous as in our day.

Today it is Hugo Chavez who is setting limousine liberals' hearts atwitter. Even as he tightened his grip on Venezuela's media and economy, silenced the press outlets he could not control, and pressured "the people" into voting to extend his tenure as president indefinitely, the usual suspects from Hollywood lined up to pay their respects and lend their credibility to the tinhorn crackpot.

In doing so, they lend global legitimacy and visibility to a man who regularly meets with North Korea's Kim Jong-il and Iran's Mahmoud Ahmadinejad.

Sean Penn, Danny Glover, and Kevin Spacey have all made the trip to see the man who is well on his way to doing for Venezuela what Robert Mugabe has done for Zimbabwe.[8]

Naomi Campbell has been to Venezuela too, but I have not yet heard whether or not it was a spiritual experience for either party.

DISHONORING OUR HEROES

I T WAS 1969, and the headline of the *Columbus Dispatch* simply read "Two Columbus GIs Killed in Vietnam." One of those fallen young men had been in the U.S. Army exactly one year to the day. Prior to his ultimate sacrifice for this great country, he spent his time as a nineteen-year-old soldier in the army of the Lord, singing and preaching the message of Christ. He was my hero—my uncle, my friend—and I miss him. In all probability, were it not for his willingness to defend freedom, I would not be writing this book today.

Don't think for a moment that Hollywood celebs or the loony Left hold a monopoly on upside-down thinking. Anyone with a fallen human nature (and that's all of us) can fall prey to it. In fact, you won't find a more twisted or offensive example in America today than that of a certain group that claims to be Christian and marches under the banner of a Baptist church.

How else can you describe a small, cultlike group of zealots who think God would have them desecrate the funerals of fallen United States servicemen in the name of making a point about homosexuality in America?

I'm referring to eighty-year-old "Reverend" Fred Phelps, who leads a small group of devoted followers (mostly family members) calling themselves Westboro Baptist Church, based in Topeka, Kansas.[1] However, Phelps isn't much of a reverend (he's a disbarred lawyer[2]), and the group doesn't function like any church I've ever seen.

Phelps and his followers are best known for showing up at the funerals of U.S. military personnel who have been killed in the line of duty. There, as grieving family and friends attempt to honor the heroism and noble sacrifice of their loved ones, Phelps and company show up shouting and holding signs with such disgusting messages as:

- "God Hates Fags"
- "Soldiers Die God Laughs"
- "God Hates Your Tears"
- "Thank God for IEDs"
- "Thank God for Dead Soldiers"[3]

(Please know these vile words are as uncomfortable for me to write as they are for you to read.)

Given their chosen obsession, you might assume that the soldiers whose funerals these loons choose to defile were homosexuals—not that that would make the group's actions one bit less detestable. Nevertheless, you would be wrong.

The fallen heroes' sexual orientation has nothing to do with Westboro's presence. In their fevered brains, every single U.S. casualty is a direct result of God's judgment on America. That judgment, they believe, is a product of God's anger over our political and cultural tolerance of homosexuality.

The fact is that Westboro throws the "God Hates Fags" line around like an advertising slogan. It is even the basis of the group's primary Web address.[4] I guess the slogan is their twisted attempt at branding—a perverse version of McDonald's "I'm lovin' it!" Nevertheless, as evidence that the group can focus its hate-filled nonsense on a variety of targets, it also registered these Web sites:

- www.godhatesamerica.com
- www.smellthebrimstone.com
- www.godhatessweden.com
- www.godhatescanada.com
- www.americaisdoomed.com
- www.godhatesireland.com[5]

Regarding the last one on that list, Phelps does not make it clear whether God's intense loathing is focused on the Republic of Ireland, Northern Ireland, or both. But clearly Phelps and his faux-Christian cult are self-styled authorities on what God hates. Wading through the muck and mire of Phelps's manifold Web sites reveals that Catholics, Jews, Episcopalians, Swedes, Kentuckians, Jerry Falwell, Fred Rogers (of *Mr. Rogers' Neighborhood*), and a long, ever-growing list of other groups and individuals are uniformly and thoroughly hated by God.

Coincidentally, God's wrath ends up also being focused on anyone who crosses Fred Phelps. Take Topeka's Blue Valley High School, for example. Prior to 2002, God, as interpreted through Phelps, didn't seem to have an opinion about Blue Valley High School. But that year Phelps announced plans to picket the school because of a drama production it was planning. On the day of the protest, a number of students cut class to meet the Westboro delegation, and an altercation ensued.

Not long after this confrontation, Phelps's Web site began carrying the message, "God Hates Blue Valley North." And so it goes. Phelps and friends have cheered Hurricane Katrina, the Indonesian tsunami, a fire that claimed the lives of several children, and pretty much every other calamity that has befallen a man, woman, or child over the past few years.

Still, it is the cult's cruel and outrageous public mockery of those who have given what Abraham Lincoln called "the last full, measure of devotion" that truly staggers the imagination. In an interview on FOX News' *Hannity & Colmes*, then cohost Sean Hannity had the following exchange with Phelps's daughter, Shirley Phelps-Roper:

> Hannity: And the fact that you use religion to justify your hatred this way, it's frankly—it's mind numbing. Do you really believe when you hold up your sign, "Thank God for IEDs," that innocent people died, "Thank God for September 11," "thank God for AIDS"...?
>
> Phelps-Roper: There are no innocent people. Yes. Thank God for 9/11. Thank God for dead soldiers. Thank God for IEDs. There are no innocent people.[6]

Virtually every Christian leader in America, myself included, has condemned Phelps's message and activities. As a lifelong student of the Bible, I can assure you that Westboro's slogan and core beliefs are completely and profoundly false. God's clear and consistent revelation of Himself—through the Bible and through His Son—is that He desperately loves every person on earth. And every one of the objects of His love (including you and me) is deeply flawed, broken, and sinful.

In other words, these moonbats have it exactly backward. And in their confusion, they purposely defile a ceremony honoring the best and bravest among us—which makes this section of this book precisely where they belong.

I've said this before, but it bears repeating here: It's not the atheist shaking his fist at the heavens that is a threat to the influence of the gospel in the earth. Far more insidious and subtle is the so-called Christian who may participate in religious rituals but who in reality is a verifiable stranger to the God he claims to serve.

There is a bit of good news emerging amid the heartache and pain caused by these deeply deceived individuals. A group of motorcyclists organized nationwide as volunteers to form a human buffer zone between mourning families and Phelps's hate-drones. They call themselves the Patriot Guard Riders, and they have been doing our nation and its grieving military families a great service. When invited to do so by the family, they physically but nonviolently keep Westboro's protestors at a respectful distance from the funeral processions.[7] I happen to love America. I respect and admire the members of its brave, patriotic military, and I own a Harley-Davidson . . . I'd like to volunteer!

Though far too many people in our nation seem to be confused or conflicted on this point, the men and women who volunteer to serve their nation are the good guys. And those who lay down their lives carrying out their duties are due every bit of honor we can pay them.

The fact that Fred Phelps not only refuses to acknowledge these truths but also indeed abuses our blood-won freedom of speech in order to torment their families tells us nothing about God. But it does reveal volumes about the man and his followers.

3

THE NEW AND IMPROVED
"HIGHEST FORM OF PATRIOTISM"

"DISSENT IS THE highest form of patriotism."

It's the pithy, if questionably accurate, phrase we heard endlessly throughout the eight years of George W. Bush's presidency. It graced the lips of numerous left-of-center talking heads on cable news chat shows and decorated the bumpers of countless Subarus, right next to the tattered "You Can't Hug With Nuclear Arms" stickers. It was also ubiquitous on the seething, angry comment threads that proliferate on Web sites like the *Huffington Post*, Daily Kos, and Democratic Underground.

Search the Congressional Record and you'll find that two Massachusetts senators (John Kerry and the late Ted Kennedy) deployed the saying while defending their tendencies to declare the war in Iraq a complete, immoral failure. Interestingly, both men attributed the quote to Thomas Jefferson, although there is no historical evidence that he said any such thing.

Yet something remarkable happened almost immediately after Barack Obama took the oath of office and Nancy Pelosi and Harry Reid gained near-super-majorities in their respective houses of Congress in January of 2009.

Suddenly, mysteriously, dissent stopped being the mark of a true patriot. In fact, overnight it became pretty much the opposite—the telltale sign of someone who is an "obstructionist" of our nation's progress toward a hopey-changey future utopia—or part of an "angry mob" and most likely a closet racist.

In the months prior to the 2008 election, we were told that anger was good. Anger was justified. Bumper stickers assured: "If you're not outraged, you're not paying attention."

In the 2006 election cycle, a lethal combination of widespread voter anger over corruption scandals, rampant pork-barrel spending, and general Bush-fatigue put Democrats back in charge of the House and Senate for the first time since 1994. Mainstream news media and the usual Hollywood suspects hailed it as a glorious popular uprising. (Compare this to Peter Jennings's famous description of the Republican takeover that swept Newt Gingrich into the Speaker's chair in 1994 as "a temper tantrum" thrown by the American people.[1])

When the 2008 elections not only put Barack Obama in the White House but also increased the majorities for House Speaker Nancy Pelosi and Senate Majority Leader Harry Reid, many left-leaning pundits declared it a historic, generational "realignment" of the American political landscape. And once again, voter anger and discontent were praised to the heavens as a powerful force for good.

So what happened? How could principled protest and grassroots citizen involvement fall so quickly from favor among the enlightened coastal opinion leaders?

Two things happened, actually: town halls and tea parties.

By the summer of 2009, grassroots resistance to the Obama-Pelosi-Reid health care proposals, along with genuine alarm over the breathtaking growth of government reach and spending, was spreading like a prairie fire across the American landscape.

Members of Congress, expecting to return to their home districts for the usual sleepy meetings attended by a half-dozen senior citizens, found themselves instead facing overflowing halls and parking lots filled with constituents eager to give them an earful.

Left-of-center politicians and pundits were quick to dismiss these raucous town halls as "astroturf"[2] operations. *Astroturfing* is the Washington beltway euphemism for a corporate lobbying effort disguised to look like a grassroots citizen movement.

With a straight face, many tried to portray the denim- and

khaki-wearing throngs carrying hand-lettered signs as corporate agents of the insurance companies. In this vein, Speaker Nancy Pelosi tried to convince a group of reporters that the crowds "are organized by out-of-district, extremist political groups, and industry-supported lobbying firms."[3]

When that didn't sell, she and others tried to paint the crowds as being angry mobs laced with neo-Nazi sympathizers. On at least one occasion, Speaker Pelosi, in answer to a reporter's question about the overflowing town hall meetings, described the crowds as both hired "astroturf" and dangerous extremists—in the same sentence![4] In other words, the "mob" was simultaneously insincere *and* crazed with angry passion. That's quite a trick.

Such outlandish and clearly ridiculous characterizations triggered widespread offense and no small measure of mirth and mockery. Consider, for example, a town hall meeting in Texas. According to an eyewitness, more than one thousand citizens stood in the August heat to hear Republican Congressman Michael Burgess (a former obstetrician) explain his opposition to the Pelosi proposal. Photographs of the event show a small, cheery grandfather in Bermuda shorts with a homemade sign pinned to his T-shirt. It featured a smiley face and read: "Hi Nancy, I'm part of the angry mob."

ABC's Charles Gibson told George Stephanopoulos, "I don't think I've ever seen this widespread pattern of angry discourse on any issue before."[5] Really? Because my memories of the Bush administration are of pretty much eight consecutive years of loud, angry discourse—beginning with "Bush was selected, not elected!" and ending with "Bush lied; people died!" and a whole bunch of "No more blood for oil!" in between.

Perhaps what Gibson meant was that he had never seen so much angry discourse from regular folks who have real jobs and who are usually too busy creating jobs, paying their bills, and paying taxes to show up at town hall meetings and cry, "Please stop the madness."

Concurrent with the town hall phenomenon, and with significant overlap, a broad, grassroots populist movement spontaneously emerged coast to coast and north to south. It began as a disorganized, bottom-up, racially and economically diverse cross section of Main Street America that came to be known as the Tea Party movement.

Once again in the liberal press, brows furrowed. "Concerns" were expressed. Hands were wrung.

As with the town hall attendees, media elites and the folks running the show in Washington seemed incapable of imputing good faith or decent motives to the Tea Party activists.

New York Times columnist Thomas Freidman compared the national atmosphere of protest fueling the Tea Party rallies to that in Israel before the assassination of Yitzhak Rabin.[6] When asked about the Tea Party movement, CNBC's Donny Deutsch told CNN's Joy Behar, "...They're angry...and I think there's a lot of racism underneath it..."[7] Rachel Maddow has suggested that the Tea Party protesters are simply tools of the pharmaceutical industry[8] and has likened the Tea Party convention to a Ku Klux Klan rally.[9]

On and on it goes—the sudden sense of alarm and fear because people are criticizing the president, some of them doing so in harsh terms.

Apparently a large number of folks in the media and on Capitol Hill slept through the eight years of the Bush presidency. I didn't. I remember the big, traffic-snarling protests. I remember the "Bush = Hitler" signs. I remember the portrayals of President Bush as a chimpanzee or, as I have already noted, a wannabe dictator.

Most of all I remember how hatred for everything related to the Bush government led to one of the most shameful episodes of that era. I'm referring to an ad placed in the *New York Times* by the group MoveOn .org on the sixth anniversary of the 9/11 attacks.

The now infamous "General Petraeus or General Betray Us?" ad (text provided on page 23) quickly became known as one of the biggest backfires in the history of political activism. One reason for the intense blowback is that the ad contained a truly outrageous smear of a genuine American hero.

The attacks on General David Petraeus truly represented a new low—and that is really saying something. To understand just *how* low, you have to have some familiarity with General Petraeus's résumé.

David Howell Petraeus graduated from the U.S. Military Academy in 1974. In 1983, the U.S. Army Command General Staff College granted him the General George C. Marshall Award for being the top graduate in his class. He later earned MPA and PhD degrees in international relations from Princeton University's Woodrow Wilson School of Public and International Affairs. As assistant professor of international relations, Petraeus also served as an educator for the U.S. Military Academy. In addition, he completed a fellowship at Georgetown University.

General Petraeus has received countless awards and decorations, including the Defense Distinguished Service Medal, two Distinguished Service Medals, two Defense Superior Service Medals, four Legion of Merit awards, the Bronze Star for valor, the State Department Superior Honor Award, the NATO Meritorious Service Medal, and the Gold Award of the Iraqi Order of the Date Palm.

On top of all that, in 2005 (two years before he took charge of military operations in Iraq) he was recognized by the *U.S. News and World Report* as one of America's "25 Best Leaders."[10]

Furthermore, the general was and is utterly nonpolitical—enjoying decades of regard and esteem from members of both political parties.

In short, the soldier unanimously confirmed by the Senate a few months earlier and summoned to Congress on September 10, 2007, to report on the progress of the troop "surge" in Iraq was one of the most highly decorated and widely respected military men in America. This man of demonstrated valor, honor, integrity, and dedication to his country was ready to, in his words, "provide as comprehensive and as forthright an assessment as we can at that time of the progress that has been achieved, and where we've fallen short."[11]

But that very morning, before General Petraeus had spoken one word of sworn testimony, he and hundreds of thousands of other Americans would open the *New York Times* to find that one of the most virulently partisan groups in America had taken out a full-page ad to declare him a traitor and a liar.

The ad read:

> General Petraeus or General Betray Us? Cooking the Books for the White House
>
> General Petraeus is a military man constantly at war with the facts. In 2004, just before the election, he said there was "tangible progress" in Iraq and that "Iraqi leaders are stepping forward." And last week Petraeus, the architect of the escalation of troops in Iraq, said, "We say we have achieved progress, and we are obviously going to do everything we can to build on that progress."
>
> Every independent report on the ground situation in Iraq shows that the surge strategy has failed....General Petraeus will not admit what everyone knows; Iraq is mired in an unwinnable religious civil war....[12]

Even solidly left-of-center publications felt compelled to disavow the attack. *Rolling Stone* magazine wrote: "For God's sake, it's not even clever. A bad pun driving a despicable message."[13] The *Boston Globe* called it "MoveOn.org's McCarthy moment."[14] And the *Washington Post's* "Fact Checker" column found numerous problems with the assertions of the ad.[15]

Ultimately, both houses of Congress voted by huge margins to condemn the smear, and the *New York Times* admitted that it had violated its own advertising policies in deeply discounting the rate MoveOn.org was asked to pay to place the ad.

Well, history has a way of making fools of the foolish. As it turned out, it was MoveOn.org that was "at war with the facts." In the months that followed General Petraeus's testimony, it became stunningly evident to all but those most completely invested in the idea of American defeat in Iraq that the general was telling the truth—and that MoveOn.org had smeared a decent and honorable American warrior in the name of petty partisan politics.

In fact, within two months, the assessment General Petraeus delivered to Congress—or at least attempted to deliver amid screaming Code Pink protestors and bloviating Democratic senators[16]—had become the consensus view. At that point, Bush Derangement Syndrome (BDS) sufferers were so invested in seeing Bush fail that they viewed victory in Iraq for our troops and a sliver of hope of a decent life for the Iraqi people as unacceptably bad news. Therefore, they simply changed the subject. Iraq began to disappear from mainstream media newscasts. (Good news is no news, I guess.)

So, how did we come to this? How does a travesty like MoveOn.org's "Betray Us" ad happen in the first place? How is a group financed by multibillionaire George Soros and others of his stripe able to publicly throw sludge at a man like David Petraeus and feel smug and righteous about it—even after being proven wrong in almost all of their assertions?

It is possible only because, to the vast majority of rage-drunk members of MoveOn.org (as well as many loyal readers and contributors at Web sites like Daily Kos, Democratic Underground, and the *Huffington Post*), everything is now *political*. There is nothing in either the public or private spheres that is not wholly about the us vs. them struggle for political power.

This extreme politicization of even our national security is a fairly new phenomenon.

Back in 1939 and 1940, Charles Lindbergh and his fellow members of the America First movement were very vocal and passionate about their belief that the United States should stay out of the budding world war between Britain and Germany. Most were isolationists. Many had pro-German sympathies. But when America was attacked on December 7, 1941, they set all that aside and went to work on behalf of victory.

Not so in the twenty-first century! With an attack on our own soil behind us and our soldiers in harm's way, a well-financed and highly visible group felt free to question the integrity and patriotism of the good man who was leading them—and felt arrogantly self-righteous in doing so.

That's upside-down thinking.

And you'll have to pardon me if I don't join those in the mainstream media who think that political discourse in this country suddenly became poisoned and ugly when President Obama took the oath of office.

Remember: dissent used to be the highest form of patriotism with these folks. But not anymore. Now, apparently, if we can't cheer for everything the government proposes to do, we are expected to keep our mouths shut.

They must be working on a new bumper sticker—one that reads: "Assent is the highest form of patriotism."

4

AMERICAN IDOLATRY

ALF A DOZEN news helicopters and a single-engine Cessna were circling over the mansion on King's Road, just off Sunset Boulevard in Los Angeles, in a kind of slow-motion aerial ballet. News trucks from ABC, CBS, NBC, CNN, FOX News, the BBC, and a dozen other international news bureaus lined the street, with microwave antennae pointing skyward, as hundreds of other gawker-packed cars jockeyed for position.

Just outside the gates of the mansion, a cross between a circus and a spring-break beach party boiled and swirled with giddy humanity. Across America, roughly half of the 150 cable channels available in most homes were prepared to interrupt regular programming and break in with a report.

Had a twentieth 9/11 hijacker been revealed and arrested? Had Jimmy Hoffa's body been discovered in a Beverly Hills backyard? Was a cure for AIDS rumored to be announced at any moment?

No.

The frenzy was because one Miss Paris Hilton was scheduled to leave her house and appear in a Los Angeles County court regarding a reckless driving citation. A breathless nation waited to catch a glimpse of her as she drove by, hopeful to discern something about her feelings from her facial expression.

Miss Hilton's face is one of the most recognized in the world. In other words, she is famous.

For most of human history, fame resulted from having done something noteworthy. Some sort of talent or achievement was pretty much prerequisite of fame—but no longer. Today being famous means only one thing: you have a face or name that is recognizable to large numbers of people. Period. Fame tells you nothing about a person.

You wouldn't know it by observing huge swaths of American and British culture today.

The sad fact is, postmodern, post-Christian society hasn't stopped being religious. The culture has simply replaced the old God with new gods. The new cathedrals and houses of worship are concert arenas and multiplexes. Inside you'll find masses of misguided people who assume famous folks are smarter, wiser, happier, and generally more special than the rest of us.

They're not.

The truth is that many, though not all, celebrities could not give an honest affirmative answer to the question "Are you smarter than a fifth grader?" Quite a few are fools in the purest, crystalline, biblical sense of the term. Many are genuinely unpleasant, dysfunctional people. In fact, according to a recent scientific study, celebrities tend to die prematurely at a rate two times higher than the general population, in many cases because they are so prone to adopting self-destructive lifestyles.[1]

And an astonishing majority of famous folks—particularly in the pop culture realms of motion pictures, television, and music—loudly hold political opinions that are, to be charitable, misguided.

Nevertheless, being the objects of adoration isn't entirely their fault.

The ones truly guilty of upside-down thinking are those who (literally) idolize famous people. I'm talking about the growing millions of *People*-magazine-reading, *MTV Cribs*–watching, would-you-please-get-a-life pop culture addicts who are making celebrity worship the fastest-growing religion in the world.

Even though it may be growing faster than ever before, it's been around for a very long time. I remember that while I was still relatively new at pastoring, a lady in our congregation asked for prayer in one of our services. She made her request with such earnestness that I thought surely a family member or dear friend was at the point of death. When I asked her to articulate her need, she requested that the congregation pray for a character on a popular afternoon soap opera—not the actress portraying the character, but the fictional character herself. In that instance, fantasy had actually become reality.

Psychologists have actually come up with a label for this behavior. They call it Celebrity Worship Syndrome (CWS for short). According to one university study in Florida, a full third of us are afflicted with the ailment to some degree,[2] and some have it really bad.

This soul-withering malady was certainly on display in the aftermath of Michael Jackson's tragic death, and before that when he was on trial for child molestation in Los Angeles County.

On that June day in 2005 when the Jackson verdict was anticipated, virtually every media outlet in the country broke away to cover the announcement. Tens of thousands of fans gathered at the courthouse and outside Jackson's Neverland ranch. Other groups huddled in cities across the nation while millions of others sat glued to their television sets. Then the word came forth: "Not guilty."

Not since an expectant throng in Times Square received news that Adolf Hitler had been defeated have we seen such rejoicing, weeping, laughing, crying, and dancing. Sadly, America's obsession with the famous has only deepened since then.

The Celebrity Worship Syndrome pandemic has made celebrity gossip Web sites like TMZ.com and PerezHilton.com some of the most heavily trafficked on the Internet. And the public's insatiable appetite for photos and videos of celebrities just trying to live their lives fuels the frenzied packs of paparazzi that stalk the stars' every move.

That is a mania with a dark side. More than one observer has suggested that a clear line of connection can be drawn between the tabloid-purchasing masses in grocery store checkout lines and the crushed Mercedes automobile in which Princess Diana lost her life on a dark Paris night.

While millions and millions of Americans obsess over whom Jennifer Aniston is dating, what Britney Spears is wearing, when Justin Timberlake got home last night, where Brad and Angelina went on vacation, and how much Nicole Richie doesn't weigh—there are people among us who are quietly doing heroic things daily and making the world a better place in which to live. These are the people deeply deserving of our admiration and emulation, yet you almost certainly have never heard of them.

For example, does the name Norman Borlaug ring a bell? No?

Don't feel too bad. Most people don't recognize the name. When Borlaug died in 2009, he was a mere ninety-five-year-old agronomist credited with breakthroughs that kept at least one billion people from starving over the last several decades. Yep, he was a full-fledged member of the "Billion Lives Saved" club—an organization with a very short membership list.[3]

Borlaug was awarded the Congressional Gold Medal by President Bush in 2007. He added this honor to his Nobel Peace Prize and his Presidential Medal of Freedom. On that day he joined Mother Teresa, Elie Wiesel, Nelson Mandela, and Martin Luther King Jr. as the only people in history to have been awarded all three.[4]

In an article for *Newsweek*, Jonathan Alter pointed to the man to illustrate just how upside down our national cult of celebrity has become. He wrote:

> Borlaug's success in feeding the world testifies to the difference a single person can make. But the obscurity of a man of such surpassing accomplishment is a reminder of our culture's surpassing superficiality.... Great scientists and humanitarians were once heroes and cover boys. No more. For Borlaug, still vital at 93, to win more notice, he would have to make his next trip to Africa in the company of Angelina Jolie.[5]

Apparently the Western world can't be bothered to take notice of extraordinary genius applied for the good of mankind. Our energies must instead be focused obsessively on which club Paris partied in last night and which designer's shoes Posh was seen wearing.

And these ladies' contributions to the good of mankind have been precisely... what?

I know a man whose life's work takes him into some of the most dangerous and unsavory places on the earth to document the horrors of human trafficking and to offer a message of hope and material help to those who are trapped in a vicious lifestyle of slavery, sex, drugs, and death. He has been threatened, harassed, and even shot for his efforts to bring freedom to some of the most victimized and abused people on the planet, but none of these things stop him or even slow him down.

I have heard firsthand the testimony of those whose family members were raped, maimed, or slaughtered just because they were of a different religion than their persecutors. I have talked to men who were carried away into captivity as children by brutal taskmasters and made to work from sunup to sundown, suffering beatings and threats that defy imagination.

I have witnessed congregations of people stand in the burned-out shell of what used to be their church and lift their hands to heaven in thanksgiving to God in the midst of tragedy that would cause less stalwart people to question whether God even existed.

I know a man in Darfur who has risked his life countless times to rescue women and children who have been kidnapped and sold into slavery. I know a pastor of an underground church in China who has been imprisoned and beaten many times for his commitment to his faith and his congregation. I have witnessed the extraordinary courage of men and women in northern Uganda in the face of the unspeakable horrors of genocide.

These and countless other unsung heroes lead the kinds of lives that should be inspiring us and providing us with examples we should hope to follow.

Instead, the average young person today aspires merely to be famous. Not to achieve, not to create, not to contribute, but to be one of the new celebrity gods. The rise of the ever-present reality shows now holds out the promise that regular folks *can* become celebrities—at least for a few weeks. All one has to do to achieve such fame is abandon all dignity, privacy, and decency.

Of course, if you can't get on a reality show, there is another path to fame. Back in 1968, the freshly arrested Sirhan Sirhan revealed it when he declared: "They can gas me, but I am famous; I have achieved in one day what it took Robert Kennedy all his life to do."[6]

By today's twisted standards, Sirhan was a success. This is upside-down-itude and backward-ity gone to seed!

STUCK IN THE '60S

A FEW DAYS AGO my lovely wife, Joni, came sad-faced into our living room and announced, "It's official; I've been the wife of your youth, and now I'm the wife of your old age." She then revealed her fresh-from-the-mailbox AARP card celebrating her fiftieth birthday. She was born in 1960...and the beat goes on.

There's an old Bruce Springsteen song that's built around the common tendency of older-middle-aged people to look back on their high school and college years as a golden age—one in which they were strong, free, and truly magnificent. It's called "Glory Days."

For many of the fifty- and sixty-somethings who now fill the upper echelons of our nation's media, academia, and government, those glory days were the 1960s. It was an era in which idealistic youths, raised in unprecedented postwar prosperity and comfort, chug-a-lugged (or should I say, smoked) an intoxicating mix of rebellion, revolutionary rhetoric, and warmed-over Marxist nonsense—all dressed up in the flower-spangled robes of Eastern mysticism and set to the music of Woodstock.

Those were heady times to be young. What galvanized all the fun was the fact that there was something to protest. There was an issue about which a nation of young people could get one another wonderfully outraged.

There was a war being waged, and in the view of many between the ages of seventeen and twenty-seven at the time, America was the bad guy.

America was the bad guy because it was fighting to stop the spread of Communism. For a group that tended to admire Mao Tse-Tung, Fidel Castro, and Che Guevara, that was a pretty dubious objective. America was the bad guy because it was wealthy and powerful and capitalistic. Ultimately, the war was bad simply because all war was bad. The concept of a "just war" was but a Christian myth. The Christian era was ending. The "Age of Aquarius" was dawning. The prophets in the musical *Hair* had decreed and declared it.

To those caught up in the fever, simple logic dictated that if war was evil, those who willingly fought it were evil too. Sure, most of the men fighting in Vietnam had been drafted, but surely they had options. They could have burned their draft cards and fled to Canada as others had. Instead, they had *chosen* to become pawns of the so-called military industrial complex.[1]

And, oh, my peace symbol, what about those who had actually enlisted? What of those who heard and answered the same call of duty their fathers and older brothers had heeded in World War II in the forties and in Korea in the fifties?

Well, they were, at best, monsters.

Countless Vietnam veterans have recounted how demoralizing it was to be in harm's way half a world away from home and hear news reports of protesters calling you a baby killer and war criminal.

For example, an April 2000 report on PBS's *NewsHour* described the experiences of two Vietnam veterans:

> Many servicemen and women returning from war did get a reaction when they returned—and it was not always pleasant. Some were blocked in airports as they waited for their return flights home. Others endured jeers and taunts from war protesters.
>
> It was that kind of treatment Tom Corey saw his fellow veterans endure, although [he] didn't face jeers himself. When Corey came back from Vietnam, nobody thought he would survive.
>
> Corey had been drafted in 1966 out of Detroit, Michigan at the age of 21. He was serving with the First Cavalry Division when he was shot during a firefight in January 1968. The bullet severed his jugular vein and hit his spinal cord. He spent years in rehabilitation.
>
> From his hospital bed, Corey watched the antiwar movement grow on television. And he couldn't believe what he saw.
>
> "I was angry at the people protesting the war," he said. "I just felt the [protesters'] energies were directed the wrong way...calling us

things that a lot of us weren't—baby killers and all of that."

For Corey, those shouting at returning servicemen were not only mocking the men in front of them, but also those that remained on Vietnam's battlefields. "I left friends behind, and I never found out what happened to them. And I lost a lot of friends," Corey said. "When I did return and watch the TV and what was going on, I was very angry."[2]

The systematic demonization of American servicemen in Vietnam represents a truly shameful chapter in our nation's history. Nevertheless, for an influential segment of an entire generation, it represents the glory days. Those days were just fond memories until, in 2003, a new Nixon (George W. Bush) aided by a new McNamara (Donald Rumsfeld) launched a new war.

Suddenly, the good old times were back. There were protests and rallies to plan, press conferences to hold, government policies to condemn, and "power" to "speak truth to." Joan Baez was dragged out of the musical closet and dusted off for atmosphere.

It was a rolling forty-year class reunion of the counterculture.

Tragically, along with this opportunity to relive their youth came the old tendency to smear our soldiers.

Of course, wars are fought by fallible human beings under unspeakably difficult circumstances. Every U.S. war has produced some instances of fog-of-war mistakes, some tragedies of poor judgment, and sadly, some truly criminal atrocities. But these have never been reflective of our forces as a whole—and they still aren't.

However, if your goal is to delegitimize a war in the eyes of the nation, you must not only undermine your neighbors' beliefs in the *aims* of the war, but you must also subvert their confidence in the *way* it is being waged. That means depicting war crimes as widespread and commonplace, even when they are not.

That is what the John Kerrys, Jane Fondas, and Tom Haydens did very successfully in the 1960s and early 1970s. And it is precisely what we saw in increasing measure as the war in Iraq unfolded.

Take the late Congressman John Murtha, for example. Though Murtha was a former Marine who should have known better than to rush to judgment about a battlefield incident, he was quick to accuse Marines in Iraq of having "killed innocent civilians in cold blood."[3] This was his assessment following reports of a battle in Haditha in which twenty-four Iraqis were killed. A thorough investigation by the Marine Corps ultimately cleared the Marines, but not before Murtha and a host of other passionate antiwar types had seized upon the incident as Iraq's version of the My Lai massacre of 1968, an event which helped turn public opinion against the Vietnam War.

Later, at least one of the smeared Marines sued Murtha for defamation.[4]

On HBO's *Real Time with Bill Maher*, actor Tim Robbins, speaking of U.S. troops in Iraq, declared: "We've killed over 400,000 of their citizens."[5]

He was wildly wrong, of course. Even the most pessimistic and anti-American counters of civilian deaths in Iraq were putting the figure at less than seventy-eight thousand[6] at the time of Robbins' accusation, and that number included civilian deaths perpetrated by terrorist suicide bombers. In other words, Robbins took the highest number of civilian deaths available, one that blames the American military for al Qaeda and insurgent marketplace bombings, and multiplied it by a factor of five.

Around the same time, the *New Republic* magazine began publishing a series of dispatches by a soldier writing under the name Scott Thomas. The Baghdad Diarist, as the magazine called him, grabbed the nation's attention when he related stories depicting himself and his fellow soldiers behaving barbarically.

In an installment under the headline "Shock Troops," Thomas, who was later revealed to be Private Scott Thomas Beauchamp, described an incident in a mess hall in which he and his fellow soldiers mocked and made fun of a woman whose face had been horribly disfigured by a roadside bomb. He wrote of a fellow soldier finding the top portion of a child's skull in a mass grave and wearing it like a hat for the rest of the day. He also described a driver of an armored vehicle who liked to intentionally run over dogs.[7]

While none of the incidents described rose to the level of war crimes, they did paint the typical American soldier as some sort of callous sociopath. Such a depiction fit the preset view of the *New Republic* and the antiwar Left to a tee.

The problem is that little, if any of it, was true. When the Army investigated these assertions of conduct unbecoming a soldier, Private Beauchamp retracted or recanted most of what he had written.[8] It seems he was just an aspiring journalist hoping to please a left-of-center audience eager to have their biases validated.

In a similar way, mainstream media have been quick to relay any story that fits the preferred narrative of bloodthirsty, brutal Americans run amok—no matter how dubious the source or how far-fetched the claims.

On the campaign trail, then Senator Barack Obama described the American military in Afghanistan as "just air-raiding villages and killing civilians."[9] The sixties' Woodstock icon David Crosby (of Crosby, Stills, Nash, and Young) told *Hardball's* Chris Matthews that when typical, patriotic American kids enter the military, they're told, "...we've gotta go in there to protect your mother and your sister. And he goes over and he finds out the job is killing somebody else's mother and sister."[10]

Eason Jordan, the head of CNN's news division, left listeners speechless when he suggested that the U.S. military had been killing journalists on purpose. In a panel discussion in Switzerland, Jordan was quoted as saying he "knew of about 12 journalists who had not only been killed by American troops, but had been targeted as a matter of policy."[11] He later backpedaled from the outrageous accusation and eventually resigned.

Later, Senator Dick Durbin took to the floor of the Senate, read some unsubstantiated accounts of prisoner treatment at Guantanamo Bay, and said: "If I read this to you and did not tell you that it was an FBI agent describing what Americans had done to prisoners in their control, you would most certainly believe this must have been done by Nazis, Soviets in their gulags or some mad regime—Pol Pot or others—that had no concern for human beings."[12]

To be fair, Senator Durbin later retracted and apologized for his comments, but not before they had been aired over and over again with Arabic translations on Al Jazeera television and repeated ad nauseum throughout the Arab-speaking world. In fact, nearly every slander and smear against our military is broadcast to our enemies and to those people worldwide whom we are trying to persuade to stand against Islamofascist extremism. Thus, these slanders are triply damaging: they undermine the morale of our fighting men and women, encourage our enemies, and alienate the neutral or undecided.

When I hear of this kind of disrespect toward our men and women in uniform, I am always reminded of the selfless sacrifices of men like my father, who fought in the frozen fields of Korea a generation ago. I think of my dear uncle, who, the last time I saw him alive, waved and wept from an airplane window on his way to Vietnam. He was returned to us in a flag-draped coffin, and his shattered body was lowered into a grave in the bedrock of a Kentucky mountainside. And I can't forget the many sons and daughters and husbands and wives who are serving right now in some of the most dangerous places in the world to protect the liberty their accusers treat with such callous disregard.

The unfair smears and slanders leveled against our troops in recent years would fill a book. And so would the countless untold stories of heroism, compassion, decency, and self-sacrifice that our military personnel have quietly lived as they have served their nation with over-whelming bravery and honor.

BLAMING THE VICTIM: ISRAEL AS SCAPEGOAT

"M USLIMS AND ARABS hate America and Europe because of Israel." "If Israel didn't exist, we wouldn't have all these problems with terrorists." "Israel's neighbors are hostile and angry because of its treatment of the Palestinians."

These "truths" have been repeated so often in so many forms that they have become articles of faith for large numbers of people who don't even, for a moment, question their validity.

There's just one problem with the conventional wisdom. It's standing on its head.

Benjamin Netanyahu nailed it when he said, "… it is not that [the Islamic world] hates the West because of Israel. *It is that they hate Israel because of the West…*" (emphasis added).[1]

You see, Israel is an island of Western democratic civilization in an increasingly medieval-fascist sea. Israel is modern and functional and allows its women to walk around not like they're the property of their husbands but as full-fledged human beings—an observance not lost on my wife, who lovingly but often sternly reminds me that God created Eve from Adam's rib, not from under his feet.

For sixty years now this little outpost of modernity has served as a living, prospering affront to every bitter Muslim who has to look back eight hundred years to recapture "the good old days."

Israel was attacked by its neighbors on the day it was founded. It has been attacked repeatedly in the years since. Only two of the surrounding Arab nations have even come close to recognizing Israel's right to exist.

The tiny democracy has been the ongoing target of the most appalling campaign of terrorism the world has ever seen.

Nevertheless, if the wildest Islamofascist fantasies became reality and Israel ceased to exist tomorrow, you can be certain that her haters would find a thousand reasons to continue hating the West and desiring its destruction. There are plenty of thousand-year-old grievances waiting in the wings to be trotted out as justification for blowing up a pizza parlor somewhere.

Nothing has served to stop a rapidly rising tide of anti-Israel hatred around the world—a tide infused with the ancient bigotry of anti-Semitism. And as usual, when someone organizes an upside-down, self-destructive-thinking parade, the UK and Europe elbow each other to get out in front of it.

For example, on Britain's National Holocaust Remembrance Day in 2003, a shocking cartoon was featured in *The Independent*; it depicted a naked Ariel Sharon (then the Israeli prime minister) eating a Palestinian baby.[2] (There's that charming, subtle British humor we've heard so much about.) Despite a flurry of complaints, it was named best cartoon of the year by Britain's Political Cartoon Society.

Some antiglobalization groups in Germany stopped vandalizing McDonald's restaurants long enough to openly suggest that Jews played a major role in planning the events of September 11, 2001. A book alleging that the CIA and Israel's Mossad intelligence agency conspired to plot the attacks on New York and Washington sat on the German best seller list for months.

The European Union published a poll in which they asked those oh-so-enlightened-and-cosmopolitan continentals which nation they believed to be the greatest threat to world peace. Israel won hands down, earning more votes than either North Korea or Iran.[3]

In response, former Soviet dissident Natan Sharansky begged the EU "to stop the rampant brainwashing against and demonizing of Israel before Europe deteriorates once again to dark sections of its past."[4]

And just what does Israel actually *do* that makes it such a menace? Does it have missiles aimed at world capitals? Does it have designs on

Saudi Arabian oil fields? Is it helping crazed dictators acquire nuclear weapons? No. Those are the specialties of a number of other nations that did not make the top five on the Europeans' "scary" list.

Israel's affront to the world is that it simply has the gall to insist on existing.

I've been to Israel many times, both with my pastor and mentor, Dr. Lester Sumrall, and on tours I have arranged through my own ministry. I never had to worry about rocks being thrown at our tour buses while in territory controlled by Israelis. At one stop I couldn't help but notice the difference in the vegetation as I gazed far across a valley. I asked our tour guide about it.

"The green areas you see in front of you are irrigated by Israeli farmers," he said. "Further in the distance are places that are controlled by others, and as you can see, their land is barren."

God's hand is upon Israel. And it's a good thing, because if Israel was only man's idea, instead of thriving it would have either died at birth or been murdered in infancy.

This glaring double standard as applied to Israel is not new, however. Back in 1968—right after the 1967 war in which Israel had successfully defended itself by handing the Egyptians, Jordanians, and Syrians their hats in six days—writer Eric Hoffer made the following observation in the *Los Angeles Times*:

> The Jews are a peculiar people: things permitted to other nations are forbidden to the Jews. Other nations drive out thousands, even millions of people and there is no refugee problem.... [But] everyone insists that Israel must take back every single Arab....Other nations when victorious on the battlefield dictate peace terms. But when Israel is victorious it must sue for peace. Everyone expects the Jews to be the only real Christians in this world.[5]

Hoffer recognized way back then that Israel, unique among all the nations of the earth, was expected *not* to defend itself. And with that expectation in mind, the posture of Hezbollah and Hamas and other terrorist groups has basically been to say to Israel, "If you do not allow us to kill you, then—well, we'll kill you." Talk about being stuck between a rock and a hard place....

And what of the Palestinians and their dream of a homeland? Pity the Palestinian people, not for being in proximity to Israel, but rather for consistently choosing and supporting the most corrupt, inept, and shortsighted leaders in history.

The fact is, every time the Israeli government has offered the Palestinians the bulk of what they want—as when Israeli Prime Minister Ehud Barak offered Yasser Arafat a "viable, contiguous Palestinian state"[6] in 2000—the Palestinians refuse and walk away. Why? Because there is only one *real* objective. It is the same one Iran's lunatic Hitler-wannabe promotes every time he gets in front of a microphone: it is to see "Israel wiped off the map."

Meanwhile, even as most of Palestine has descended into a civil war between Fatah and Hamas factions, they remain the darlings of the Western media and our so-called intellectuals. As Canadian columnist Mark Steyn has observed:

> If I were a Palestinian, I'd occasionally wonder what I had to do to get a bad press. Elect a terrorist government explicitly committed to the destruction of Israel? No, no, no, don't jump to conclusions, explains Bill Clinton. It's just a vote for better municipal services. Send my daughter to explode in an Israeli restaurant? Oh, well, shrug the experts, it's an act born of "desperation" and "frustration." You have to remember Palestinians don't have any tanks, so they have to make do with what the mayor of London's favorite imam calls "the children bomb."[7]

While the terrorists get a free pass, the blame-the-victim trend grows stronger. Those who used to only whisper about undue "Jewish influence" and the power of "the Israel lobby" now feel free to write and speak openly.

Of the many signs pointing to the fact that Western culture has a near-fatal case of backward thinking, none is more glaring or chilling than the increasing tendency to make Israel and the Jews the scapegoat for nearly everyone's problems, nearly everywhere.

PHONY OUTRAGE

I N THE BIBLE'S Book of Proverbs, one of the wisest men who ever lived wrote, "He who digs a pit will fall into it, and he who rolls a stone, it will come back on him."[1] What old King Solomon suggests here is that people who set a trap for others often end up in it themselves.

Back in September of 2007, Senate Majority Leader Harry Reid dug a pit in hopes of trapping Rush Limbaugh. Instead it was Reid who ended up in the pit. Then a stone rolled in on him. Then the stone exploded.

In the history of absurd accusations, few could top the attempt by Reid and a wild-eyed mob of partisan, liberal Limbaugh-loathers to tar the radio commentator as being "against the troops."

Anyone vaguely familiar with Limbaugh's positions and history found the accusation about as credible as accusing Lindsay Lohan of being against nightclubs. But desperate times call for desperate measures. And in late September, the antiwar Democrats and their leader were desperate.

Beginning on September 10, 2007, the day MoveOn.org ran a full-page ad in the *New York Times* suggesting that General David Petraeus was a traitor and a liar (see chapter 3, "The New and Improved 'Highest Form of Patriotism'"), the antiwar, anti-Bush, anti-victory-in-Iraq crowd had been under withering fire from conservatives, particularly radio talk show hosts and Internet bloggers. Indignant Republicans were calling on Democrats to condemn the MoveOn.org ad, but Reid and the Dems knew they couldn't do so without offending the pitchfork-and-torch-carrying far-left wing of their support base. Besides, one off-the-record senator had already let it slip that he and his colleagues were using MoveOn.org to do the dirty work they couldn't be seen by the public to be doing.

Those concerns proved to be well founded. Most polls showed the

American public didn't think highly of the Petraeus smear, either. The approval ratings of the Democrat-led Congress—already even lower than President Bush's historically low ratings—were sinking by the day. They hit 11 percent on September 19, to be precise.[2] To put it in perspective, that's a lower level of approval than that of athlete's foot, tick bites, or that annoying commercial that used to shout endlessly, "Apply directly to the forehead!"

Of course, when you've done something stunningly, breathtakingly stupid with the whole world watching, and people won't stop talking about it, it's only human nature to try to change the subject. And it's even better if you can do so by pointing everyone to someone who is even worse than you are.

Thus, on September 28, Reid and company took to the floor of the Senate and the House to condemn Rush Limbaugh for something he had said two days earlier on his radio program. The source of their outrage was a liberal media monitoring Web site called Media Matters, which had posted a story the day before under the headline: "Limbaugh: 'Service Members Who Support U.S. Withdrawal Are "Phony Soldiers."'" Under the headline, the group wrote: "During the September 26 broadcast of his nationally syndicated radio show Rush Limbaugh called service members who advocate U.S. withdrawal from Iraq 'phony soldiers.'"[3]

Left-leaning members of the House and Senate who had spent the previous two weeks being beaten about the head and shoulders with the MoveOn.org Petraeus debacle saw their opportunity and seized it. As one journalist described it:

> Within a few hours, a half-dozen congressional Democrats had denounced Limbaugh's remarks. "How dare Rush Limbaugh label anyone who has served in the military as a, quote, 'phony soldier?'" asked Illinois Democratic Rep. Jan Schakowsky.[4]

Rep. Chris Van Hollen, Democrat from Maryland, asserted, "Rush Limbaugh owes our military and their families an apology."[5]

Not to be outdone, Reid accused Limbaugh of attacking "those fighting and dying for him and for all of us. Rush Limbaugh got himself a deferment from serving when he was a young man. He never served in uniform. He never saw in person the extreme difficulty of maintaining peace in a foreign country engaged in a civil war. Yet he thinks that his opinion on the war is worth more than those who are on the front lines."[6]

Iowa Senator Tom Harkin took the high road—literally. He said of Limbaugh, "Maybe he was just high on his drugs again. I don't know."[7]

There is just one little problem with all this deeply heartfelt outrage and sincere sorrow for Limbaugh's scandalously low opinion of America's fighting men and women. Media Matters had completely misunderstood, or more likely, intentionally misconstrued Limbaugh's comments on his program.

The "fake soldiers" he had referred to were actually and literally fake soldiers. Two nights before Limbaugh's broadcast, ABC's *World News* with Charles Gibson had run a story that Gibson introduced with the words, "A closer look tonight at phony heroes."[8] It was about the growing phenomenon of men claiming to be veterans who are not.

The ABC piece highlighted the now infamous case of Jesse Macbeth. As *World News* reporter Brian Ross explained in the report:

> Authorities say the most disturbing case involves this man, 23-year-old Jesse Macbeth....In a YouTube video seen around the world, Macbeth became a rallying point for antiwar groups, as he talked of the Purple Heart he received in Iraq and described how he and other U.S. Army Rangers killed innocent civilians at a Baghdad mosque.[9]

Ross's report continued with a video of Macbeth saying, "Women and men, you know—while in their prayer, we started slaughtering them."[10]

Here's the problem. Macbeth was lying—about everything. He had served in the army precisely six weeks before washing out of basic training. But before that "inconvenient truth" came to light, Macbeth had become a poster boy for an American Far Left eager to paint our soldiers as monsters. (See chapter 4, "Trapped in the '60s.")

As Limbaugh explained on his program the day after being vilified in the halls of Congress, a member of his production staff had seen the report and brought it to Limbaugh's attention. In doing additional research on the story before airtime, a Limbaugh researcher also came across a story about Macbeth on FoxNews.com that had the phrase "Phony Soldier" in the headline.[11]

This phenomenon is what Limbaugh had in mind when he said what he did on his program.

Thus, Media Matters and those who followed their lead were completely off base in accusing a man with a twenty-year public record of patriotic support for the military of being the most outrageous slanderer of fighting men since a once future Massachusetts senator had testified to Congress that our soldiers in Vietnam were all a bunch of "Genghis Khans burning, raping, looting, and killing."[12]

But to Reid and his fellow members of the Surrender Caucus, it didn't matter that the horse they were trying to ride was lame with a capital *L*. It was all they had, and they were going to ride it!

Thus Reid returned to the Senate floor a day later and declared that Limbaugh had gone "way over the line." In his continued remarks, Reid said, "This comment was so beyond the pale of decency that it cannot be left alone."[13] Then he and forty other Democratic senators signed a letter to Mark May, the CEO of Clear Channel Communications, the corporate distributor of Limbaugh's program. The letter called on May "to publicly repudiate [Limbaugh's] comments."[14]

Fortunately, May knew nonsense-on-stilts when he saw it. He wrote a public reply to the senators, which included these excerpts:

> Given Mr. Limbaugh's history of support for our soldiers, it would be unfair for me to assume his statements were intended to personally indict combat soldiers simply because they didn't share his own beliefs regarding the war in Iraq.
>
> ...I hope that you understand and support my position that while I certainly do not agree with all views that are voiced on our stations, I will not condemn our talent for exercising their right to voice them.[15]

This was May's diplomatic way of telling forty-one senators they could "move on" to the nearest lake and attempt a half gainer.

The controversy might have died a lingering, smelly death right there, had Limbaugh not turned the attack into one of the most brilliant and successful public relations coups in media history.

First, he acquired from his boss, Mark May, the actual condemn-o-gram bearing the forty-one senatorial signatures. He then proceeded to put it up for auction on eBay, promising to donate all sales proceeds to the Marine Corps Law Enforcement Foundation, a charity that gives scholarship assistance to children of Marines and federal law enforcement personnel who die in the line of duty. In the eBay listing, Limbaugh promised the highest bidder not only the letter but also "the Halliburton briefcase in which the letter was secured 24 hours a day, a letter of thanks from Limbaugh, and a picture of him announcing the auction at a speech in Philadelphia...."[16]

Finally, Limbaugh promised to match the high bid with a donation of his own to the same foundation.

When the bidding for the letter rapidly reached $100,000, it began to grab the nation's attention. When it surpassed the $1 million mark, it was obvious Limbaugh had taken a stunt cynically manufactured to damage him and turned it into a way to highlight his long-standing pro-military sentiments—and do some good at the same time.

As bidding headed toward $2 million, Harry Reid couldn't resist one last opportunity to make himself look artificial and pathetic. He took to the floor of the Senate one more time in the hopes of jumping on the freight train before it ran over him.

He didn't offer to match Limbaugh's donation to the fund, though he is a wealthy man. He didn't even offer to pull his forty co-signers together to divide the pain of matching the donation. No, he nobly and selflessly encouraged other people to bid on the letter because it was for a good cause.

In other words, he made a desperate and transparent attempt to glom onto the eBay juggernaut in hopes of claiming a piece of the credit for it. It was a little like Mrs. O'Leary's cow attempting to take credit for the construction boom in Chicago after the fire of 1871.

Regular Limbaugh listener Betty Casey of the Eugene B. Casey Foundation placed the winning bid of $2.1 million.[17] As promised, Limbaugh ponied up his matching gift, thereby providing a $4.2 million infusion of funds for a very important and deserving nonprofit.

Media Matters, Reid, and a host of others dug a pit. But at the end of the day, it was they who found themselves with muddy hands and red faces, looking up from the bottom of a hole.

Of course, the phony "fake soldiers" scandal was only one in what has been a long chain of attempts by powerful interests to whip up outrage in order to have Limbaugh declared a pariah and driven from the airways with pointy sticks and torches.

For example, there was much garment rending and teeth gnashing shortly after the election of Barack Obama when it was reported throughout the land that Rush Limbaugh had said that he hoped Obama would fail. This was pretty incendiary stuff during those heady days in which most Americans (myself included) were savoring the fact that, regardless of what we thought of Barack Obama's politics, America had just elected her first president of color.

When Limbaugh received a request from one of the major news magazines to submit four hundred words describing his hopes for the Obama administration, Rush pointed to the many objectionable goals and policies the candidate had articulated on the campaign trail. Limbaugh went on the air and, in his own timid, shrinking-violet way, said:

> Look, what he's talking about is the absorption of as much of the private sector by the U.S. government as possible, from the banking business, to the mortgage industry, the automobile business, to health care. I do not want the government in charge of all of these things. I don't want this to work. So I'm thinking of replying to the guy, "Okay, I'll send you a response, but I don't need 400 words, I need four: 'I hope he fails.'"[18]

Sounds reasonable to me. When George W. Bush was elected, my liberal friends certainly weren't wishing him Godspeed and smooth sailing in advancing a conservative agenda. Nor did I expect them to. What rational person would? Nevertheless, for several days following Limbaugh's broadcast, the news shows, chat shows, and Internet blogs were filled with feverish discussions of Limbaugh's comment accompanied by shrieks of horror. Scarcely a single Republican politician escaped having to respond to a reporter's question about whether he or she shared Rush Limbaugh's desire to see the new president "fail."

Of course, this controversy and the ensuing efforts to silence him have served only to raise Limbaugh's profile and boost his ratings. As always, Rush cries all the way to the bank—oddly enough, walking on his feet.

DEFINING DICTATORSHIP DOWN

I THINK IT'S FAIR to say that George W. Bush is a dictator."
This was the studied, reasoned, temperate opinion of Erica Jong, the feminist soft-core porn writer who was a guest on CNN's *Showbiz Tonight* television program.[1] Rational viewers who saw it may have thought it "fair" to conclude that somewhere along the line Ms. Jong had lost her marbles—or at minimum her grip on the definition of the word *dictator*. But she is far from alone.

In the final months of the Bush presidency, it was all the rage to confidently claim that President Bush wanted to become a dictator, had been in the process of becoming a dictator, or, as Jong asserted, *already was* a dictator. In fact, these claims had become fashionable right after the hotly litigated election results of 2000. Just check Google, where a simple search using the terms *Bush* and *dictator* yields nearly two million results.

After September 11, 2001, President Bush attempted to grapple, like a responsible adult, with one of the most complex and sobering national security challenges in our nation's history—namely, how to respond to a declared war upon us by attackers who hide within every nation on the earth, wear no uniforms, and respect none of the rules of conventional warfare or statecraft.

In that process, Bush took some commonsense steps that were mild in comparison to those enacted by Abraham Lincoln and Franklin Roosevelt (both revered presidents) in previous times of war. But these measures triggered howls that Bush was rapidly becoming the new Hitler and was willfully dismantling our democracy on behalf of corporate interests. The consistent accusation was that the war on terror was just a ruse, a device for scaring people into surrendering their freedoms. This explains the logic-defying popularity of the "9/11 was an inside job" lunacy.

Here is what actually represents a fairly moderate, reasoned example of this genre. Under a post headlined "How George Bush Became a Dictator," a Texas blogger wrote:

> Bush seems to have created a dictatorship by exploiting a national tragedy, by manipulating a wave of fear, by fanning the flames of racial and religious prejudice. He divided the world into two opposing camps: us and "evil-doers" and declared that if you disagreed with him, then you, too, were an "evil-doer." Declaring that he did not do *nuance*, Bush made of stupidity a virtue. He suppressed dissent and declared himself above the law.[2]

Professional gadfly Ralph Nader provided further evidence that he is unhinged at any speed when he suggested that the president was acting "in effect as a selected dictator.... For a cheap political advantage, the administration will destroy freedoms and civil rights, undermine our economy and destroy the position of the United States in the world."[3]

Harry Belafonte limbo-ed down to Venezuela and, once and for all, answered the question "How low can you go?" He told unapologetic Marxist President Hugo Chavez: "No matter what the greatest tyrant in the world, the greatest terrorist in the world, George W. Bush says, we're here to tell you... [that] millions of the American people... support your revolution."[4]

This represents a twofer in upside-down thinking for Belafonte—calling a good man evil and an evil man good all in the same sentence.

Sean Penn, this generation of entertainers' upside-down answer to Bob Hope, told Larry King that President Bush had "devastated our democracy."[5] As it turns out, that was a few weeks before the Democrats reclaimed both the House and the Senate in the midterm elections, so he may have had a point.

But it's not just flame-throwing activists, actors, and wannabe pundits on the Internet who have made a practice of throwing around the word *dictator* so casually that it has become meaningless. Some serious people who ought to know better caught the fever as well.

Newsweek's Jonathan Alter wrote in December of 2005: "We're seeing clearly now that Bush thought 9/11 gave him license to act like a dictator...."[6]

And when it was reported that the National Security Agency was analyzing phone records in hopes of detecting any patterns of communication between known terrorist organizations abroad and people inside the United States (and that Senator Arlen Specter had some concerns about it), CNN's Jack Cafferty hyperventilated: "[Specter] might be all that's standing between us and a full-blown dictatorship in this country."[7]

Keep in mind, we're talking about a democratically elected president who was constantly vilified in the press and denounced in every public forum. (You know, the way dictators everywhere are freely denounced in the nations they rule.) He was a political leader who was thwarted by Congress where most of his domestic agenda was concerned and stymied by the Supreme Court in many of his antiterrorism measures. If that doesn't prove he wasn't a dictator, try this: his judicial nominees tended to stay bottled up in the Senate and his party lost majorities in both houses of Congress, while he was supposedly at the height of his dictatorial powers.

Some tyrant.

Yes, Bush was quite the power-wielding machine—a dictator in the truest sense of the word. That is, if by *dictator* you mean a well-meaning guy who maddeningly managed to barely get elected (twice) in spite of the all-out, unified efforts of the mainstream media, the entertainment industry, and special-interest groups backed by billionaires.

Well, perhaps it was Bush's legendary oratorical skills that duped the populace. Maybe he mesmerized the nation with his spellbinding speeches and golden-tongued mastery of the English language. Yes, that's it.

Somehow, during this nation's dark night of oppression and dissent crushing, Web sites like WhyWeHateBush.com, AWOLBush.com, BushLies.net, and TooStupidToBePresident.com proliferated like mushrooms. There were literally thousands of them, and yet not a single webmaster ever awakened with a severed computer monitor in his bed as a warning.

The sad irony is that, throughout this period, real dictators thrived and emerged, and without so much as a peep from the folks rending their clothing about the tyrant Bush (except, of course, for hearty peeps of praise and admiration).

One of the difficulties and dangers our culture faces is that what used to cause legitimate outrage now barely merits a nod. A generation ago if you uttered the word *abortion* in most churches, you would have been greeted by a chorus of righteous indignation. Now it has become so commonplace in our conversation and our culture that most modern churchgoers barely notice—and multitudes who have grown up with abortion as the law of the land fail to associate it with the horror it truly represents.

In the same way, when the term *dictator* is used in a calculating fashion to achieve a pre-calculated response, as it so often is today, people tend to disregard what a threat a real dictator actually is.

Russian president Vladimir Putin steadily gathered power and control to himself while, one by one, his opponents and critics died violent, mysterious deaths.

And then there was the man *New Statesman* magazine described as "possibly the world's cruellest [*sic*] autocrat."[8] North Korea's Kim Jong-Il (no relation to Erica Jong) was and is the focus of a nightmarish totalitarian cult of personality and thought-policing—a caricature of George Orwell's *1984*. In the Democratic People's Republic of Korea—a hell that is neither democratic, nor the people's, nor a republic—just being suspected of being disloyal to Dear Leader results in truly unspeakable things happening to you and your family.

This is how it is in real, rather than imagined, dictatorships.

Zimbabwe's president-for-life Robert Mugabe is known around the world for corruption, suppression of political opposition, abuse of land reform, economic collapse, and violations of human rights. Under his care the nation has gone from being a net exporter of food to being a home to mass starvation. Zimbabwe also has one of the highest inflation rates in the world, at one point predicted to hit 1.5 million percent.⁹ Yet while former President Bush quietly left the White House and returned to private life, Mugabe won't be doing so anytime soon.

Of course, I have already pointed to the affront to freedom and hope that is Castro's Cuba. (See chapter 1, "Fawning Over Thugs.")

And then there are a whole host of other real-deal tyrants currently crushing people under their boots around the world—and you probably haven't heard or seen a single news story about them in the last five years.

There is Alexander Lukashenko of Belarus, Saparmurat Niyazov of Turkmenistan, Teodoro Obiang Nguema of Equatorial Guinea, Alfredo Stroessner of Paraguay, Senior General Than Shwe of Burma, and a rogues' gallery of other brutish control freaks who have actually earned the label *dictator*. But the shameless and promiscuous use of the word by entertainers, journalists, and politicians in the service of a political agenda during the Bush years cheapened the language and soiled our civil discourse.

Of course, on January 20, 2009, in very un-dictator-like fashion, President Bush quietly vacated the White House and headed for his ranch in Crawford, Texas. As the Obama team took the reins of the executive branch in another of this nation's amazing peaceful power transfers, did Erica Jong or any of those other hysterical voices that had been declaring the end of our democracy offer an apology? Of course not.

If indeed our democracy is in danger, it is only because there are too many today who are filled with blind hatred and an easy willingness to apply a label like *tyrant* to good men and women with whom they disagree.

PALIN DERANGEMENT SYNDROME

BUSH DERANGEMENT SYNDROME *(BDS)*. I think it was *Washington Post* columnist Charles Krauthammer who first coined the phrase. It was an apt label for the extreme variety of upside-down thinking that seemed to go along with an all-consuming hatred for George W. Bush and, by extension, every initiative identified with him (including the war against al Qaeda in Iraq and the noble attempt to establish a stable beachhead of democracy in that region).

Apparently one of the long-term effects of Bush Derangement Syndrome was to destroy the centers in the human soul that create the capacity for shame. I say that because untold shameless things were said and written about the man during the eight years of his presidency. Among the victims of BDS were members of MoveOn.org, most of the Hollywood entertainment-industrial complex, the editorial boards of the *New York Times* and *Los Angeles Times*, and large majorities staffing network newsrooms and college faculties nationwide.

The list of other BDS symptoms typically included:

- Seething hatred
- Paranoia
- Unbridled cynicism
- More seething hatred
- Obsession
- Delusions of righteousness
- Even much more seething hatred

Today we seem to have a new, mutated strain of the virus on the loose, and it appears to be infecting a lot of the same folks who fell victim to the last one. It is producing Palin Derangement Syndrome and is triggered by the very existence on the planet of former Alaska Governor Sarah Palin.

From almost the very hour Senator John McCain made the surprise announcement that his pick for a running mate was a little known woman governor from faraway, sparsely populated Alaska, Sarah Palin has been the focus of intense, bizarre, and often vicious treatment by the media and the entertainment-industrial complex.

The initial media frenzy was understandable—not to mention just what the McCain campaign was hoping for. Few in news media circles knew much of anything about Governor Palin. She was a mysterious but obviously beautiful, unknown quantity. Thus there was a mad scramble to find out everything possible as quickly as possible about the woman John McCain had chosen to share his platform.

Nevertheless, the news media establishment was by that point deeply invested in the idea of Barack Obama as president. As soon as it became clear that Palin was providing a massive boost of enthusiasm and interest in the McCain candidacy, the smearing, mocking, reputation-mangling media machinery was set into motion.

A gold rush of reporters and investigators invaded sleepy Wasilla, Alaska, and started panning and digging for anyone willing to dish dirt on the town's former mayor. When it was learned, to the horror of the coastal elites, that Palin was a regular churchgoer (particularly in the wake of candidate Obama having suffered some embarrassment over comments by his former pastor), every sermon Palin's present and former pastors had ever preached was examined for exploitable statements that she could be challenged to affirm or disavow.

Tina Fey started working on her Sarah Palin impression. Soon, ugly and ridiculous conspiracy theories about the recent birth of Palin's son Trig began to seep out of the sewage pipes that run to and from the nation's most popular left-wing Web sites and blogs.

Within weeks, a blogger for the *San Francisco Chronicle* was moved to write:

> The attacks on Palin have ranged from patronizing to vicious to fantastical. She has been caricatured as an inexperienced rube, a baby-making automaton, an uneducated underachiever, a bad mother, trailer-park trash, a right-wing religious fanatic, a sexual fantasy, and, of course, a fascist. No subject has been deemed taboo in the effort to take Palin down. What her detractors don't seem to realize is that in the process of insulting Palin, they are insulting the majority of the country.[1]

However, as is often the case, their railing accusations, minted as a slur, served only to publish her true character.

McCain's loss in the general election didn't put an end to this strange and horrible obsession, though it might have if Sarah Palin had simply gone back to Alaska and resumed her former life. But she didn't.

As I sought for an explanation about all the frenzied media noise about Palin, I remembered a scene from a movie that was made so long ago that Robert Redford was still a young man. In the 1972 film *Jeremiah Johnson*, Redford had teamed up with another mountain man while traveling in the Colorado Rockies when they met a Native American of the Flathead tribe who asked them, in an extremely agitated tone, about the ponies they were riding.

"So what's he shouting for?" Johnson asked his companion.

"Scared of you," came the reply.

It's been my experience that many times the people who exhibit the greatest anger are also the ones who are the most afraid.

Although Sarah Palin stepped down as governor of Alaska, she chose to remain on the national stage. And so the love-hate relationship continues. In fact, Palin garners a level of media attention that is nothing short of astonishing for an ex-governor who was the vice-presidential nominee on a losing ticket.

No piece of news about Palin is too obscure to merit discussion and analysis. No action is so trivial that it shouldn't be mentioned, parodied, or mocked. For example, when Palin addressed the 2010 Tea Party convention in Nashville, news photographs revealed that Palin had three talking points written on her hand. The terms *Energy, Tax Cut,* and *Lift American Spirits*[2] were obviously there to serve as reminders for points she wanted to hit during the question and answer time that was scheduled to follow her speech.

The entire media world spent the next several days discussing and deriding the (literally) handwritten notes. Stand-up comics, talking news heads, and supposedly serious journalists offered deep thoughts and wisecracks about the notes. Andrea Mitchell went on the air at MSNBC with notes on her hand, to great mirth and amusement in the studio. Even President Obama's press secretary, Robert Gibbs, tried to get a few laughs from the White House press corps by showing up for the daily briefing with notes on his hand. To their credit, many of the assembled reporters just groaned and rolled their eyes.

Previously President Obama had been the focal point of some teasing for taking a teleprompter with him wherever he spoke, including for an address to a classroom of sixth graders. But not even his harshest conservative critics ever suggested that the dependence on a teleprompter was a sign of low intelligence. Nor should they have suggested such a thing.

But to many liberal bloggers, six words on Palin's hand were a clear sign of an inferior intellect. Typical of this line of "upside-down thinking" was the opening of Chris Matthews's twelve-minute-long attack on Sarah Palin that began the February 8, 2010, edition of *Hardball*:

> Can a palm reader be president? What do we think of kids in school who write stuff on their hands to get through a test? What do we think of a would-be political leader who does it to look like she's speaking without notes? What do we think of Sarah Palin this weekend answering pre-screened questions from a like-minded audience in Nashville, a tea party convention, and still having to put a cheat sheet on her palm to answer what she calls the basics of her beliefs?[3]

Matthews's marathon attack was just a part of what amounted to hundreds of hours of television airtime and billions of bytes of Internet bandwidth devoted to portraying Palin as stupid and a little dishonest for making a few notes on her hand. This made it all the more inconvenient when an enterprising researcher found a videotape of Democratic Senator Dianne Feinstein, the liberal icon from California, using notes on her hand during a debate when she was running for governor of California back in 1990.

There was just one significant difference in the two women's use of palm-inscribed talking points. For Feinstein, it was a clear violation of debate rules. Among all the major news networks, only FOX News bothered to bring the Feinstein connection to the attention of their viewers.[4]

And so it goes. As with other good people being portrayed as stupid, crazy, or evil by our upside-down culture, Sarah Palin just seems to get stronger and more successful with every nasty attack.

Her biographical book, *Going Rogue*, set sales records and sat atop the *New York Times* nonfiction list for months. The demand for her as a speaker is enormous and rising. But then so is the level of disdain felt by some of our most powerful members of media, academia, and government for Palin—and for the growing numbers of independent voters in America who find her a breath of fresh air.

SUMMARY (PART 1)

I N 1928, THE City of Philadelphia passed an ordinance granting the local Boy Scout council permission to have its headquarters on city land along with the right to lease the land on which the building sits for $1 per year "in perpetuity."

You may have missed the memo, but apparently "perpetuity" isn't what it used to be. Under pressure from national homosexual activist groups and the ACLU, the city reneged on its long-standing promise and informed the Cradle of Liberty Council of Boy Scouts that they would have to start paying $200,000 per year if they wanted to continue to use the land underneath their building.[1]

Scout troops in San Francisco and Boston have been displaced through the use of similar tactics. In fact, from sea to shining sea, one of America's oldest and best organizations has been under assault because it stubbornly puts the interests of the young men it serves above the demands of political correctness. Typically, some of the same individuals and groups that have vilified the Catholic Church for failing to protect children from sexual predators are condemning the Boy Scouts for attempting to do so.

Conservative author Heather Mac Donald, herself an atheist, recognizes how out-of-control and wrong-headed this coordinated attack on the Scouts is. She writes:

> The Scout litigation is an alarm that America's obsession with alleged discrimination has gone too far. Elite culture now sees the highest function of government as correcting the petty prejudices of the citizens, even if that means destroying civil society in the process.

> If the government's crusade against so-called bigotry means evis-
> cerating the scouts, it is long past time to shut the crusade down.
> Scouting does more good in a year than an army of ACLU lawyers
> has ever done.[2]

That an organization with the history, goals, and results of the Boy
Scouts of America is under attack in the courts, in city halls, and in the
press tells you everything you need to know about our culture's deep
confusion about who the good guys are.

As the previous eight chapters have illustrated, utterly upside-down
thinking about who deserves praise and who has earned condemnation
is rampant right now.

The question is, how did we go, in just a few generations, from being the
nation that closed ranks and pulled together in World War II—a nation
in which there was broad consensus about values, vices, and virtues—to
this hall of funhouse mirrors? How did we arrive at a place where our
war heroes are pilloried, swaggering dictators are toasted by movie stars,
and anti-Semitic paranoia is displayed openly in polite society?

More pressingly, is it possible to find our way back to sanity? Will we
find a way to remember who the good guys are once more?

I believe we can. But doing so will require following the river of confusion back to its headwaters. The reason no one can tell good guys from bad
guys anymore is that we first abandoned the concepts of *good* and *bad*.

Our cultural elites have long since "outgrown" a belief in absolute right
and wrong. Our oh-so-postmodern thinkers have convinced themselves
that truth is an illusion in the eye of the beholder. As Dennis Prager
wrote, "Most secular individuals do not confront these consequences
of moral relativism. It is too painful for most decent secular people to
realize that their moral relativism, their Godless morality, means that
murder is not really wrong, that 'I think murder is wrong,' is as meaningless as 'I think purple is ugly.'"[3]

Is it any wonder so many now feel free to tear down good men striving
to do good things?

Two thousand years ago, Jesus of Nazareth encountered a culture that had also turned a lot of truth on its head. He found people pridefully obsessing over the minutest details of arcane religious law, yet giving not a thought to God's grand command to remember the poor and oppressed. He found people looking for political fixes to their spiritual shortcomings. He found people treasuring things they should have despised and neglecting things of true and lasting value.

The apostle Paul described the decaying culture as one in which many people had "exchanged the truth of God for a lie."[4] Jesus waded into every public forum in the culture and declared, "I *am* the...truth."[5] And in each place, He gave them an opportunity to reverse that exchange—to trade deception for reality.

When Pontius Pilate encountered Jesus in the context of a phony trial, Jesus told him: "...for this reason I was born, and for this I came into the world, to testify to the truth. Everyone on the side of truth listens to me."[6]

Pilate's reaction to that frank declaration was to do what a lot of the upside-down thinkers in our day do—whip out the old freshman Philosophy 101.

"What is truth?"[7] Pilate muttered.

The unspoken answer was, "You're looking at Him."

PART 2

LIFE IS BAD...DEATH IS GOOD

OVERVIEW

I N MOST ARENAS the utter ridiculousness of upside-down thinking is at least good for some comic relief. And the last decade certainly provided some classic moments of hilarity.

I mean, watching Senator Harry Reid huff and puff in make-believe indignation about a make-believe insult to the very troops he had spent months declaring to be failures—an alleged insult by a conservative, pro-military hawk of all people...well, you just can't make that stuff up.

There is also the spectacle of the Dixie Chicks posing as brave martyrs for free speech. You'll recall they trashed our former president on foreign soil, shamelessly pandering to a Bush-hating British crowd and triggering cheers and applause. When we later heard the ladies on the talk show circuit whining about the awful price they'd paid for their convictions, even as they were toasted all over Hollywood and Manhattan and as the entertainment industry handed them every award possible, you couldn't help but laugh. (Of course, they didn't think much of personal liberty when a few million country music fans exercised their right to avoid their albums and concerts like the plague.)

And if you can't chuckle at a gaggle of preening stars, moguls, and tycoons who fly in for a global warming conference in which they reprimand regular folks for using incandescent bulbs and running their air conditioners too much, then your irony sensors must have long ago overloaded and burned out.

Speaking of global warming, another case of living on our heads was obvious when ninety-eight-year-old Irena Sendler's nomination for the Nobel Peace Prize was passed over. Irena personally managed to smuggle out and save twenty-five hundred infants and children from the Warsaw ghetto during the Nazi occupation in World War II. She was caught and had her legs and arms broken by her captors.[1] The Nobel selection committee chose someone they regarded as more worthy of the peace prize—Al Gore for his slide show on global warming. What used to be most important obviously isn't any more.

As an English novelist once wrote, "Nothing is a matter of life and death except life and death."[2] That's why inverted thinking gets a lot less funny when it is applied to birth, death, human life, and medical ethics—areas that are home to some of the most stunning wrong-headedness on earth.

Make no mistake; we're living in an era of rampant perversity in our views of life and death. So it should not surprise us to learn that, in an age of widespread confusion about the value of life, death has become chic. As the trendsetters in New York's East Village might say, "Morbid is the new black."

It used to be said that art imitated life, and vice versa. Now even that has been turned on its head. Now art imitates death. In fact, many of the most celebrated "modern" artists work in body parts and cadavers instead of oils, watercolors, or clay as their medium of choice.

A widely known example of "death art" is the controversial Body Worlds exposition by Gunther von Hagens, which a *Boston Globe* headline rightly described as a "traveling cadaver show."[3] The accompanying article went on to say:

> The 61-year-old physician, university lecturer, and anatomist-cum-artist's exhibitions of plasticized, partially dissected bodies—an expectant mother cross-sectioned to reveal her unborn child, a man peeled to his musculature, carrying his skin like an old raincoat—hover somewhere between the sublime and the unspeakable.[4]

Dr. Hagens's mobile chamber of horrors is only the most recent and spectacular example of the trend toward calling whatever is shocking, revolting, or grotesque *art*. As early as the mid-1990s you had the *New York Times*'s art critics offering glowing reviews filled with paragraphs like this one:

> Ms. Matalon's sculptures also feel personal but in a tough, impacted way. Molded from wire, wax, tar, and gauze, they resemble butchered human body parts—suspended breasts in one case, severed legs propped up against the gallery wall in another—made abstract by the very process of decay.[5]

Ummm...right.

Then there is the music scene. In an environment of increasing fragmentation and declining sales, the musical genre (and I use the term *musical* very loosely) generally known as *death metal* is going stronger than ever. Even in this hyper-niche-y marketplace for music, new death metal albums routinely appear on the Billboard Top 200 Albums list.[6]

In recent years, the hellish maw of death metal has spawned a dozen or more subgenres. Among the ones listed under the article on "Death Metal" in the online encyclopedia Wikipedia, we find: melodic death metal, technical death metal, progressive death, deathgrind, grindcore, death-thrash, brutal death, death/doom, and blackened death metal. (That final entry may or may not describe a style that employs the use of Cajun spices. I'm afraid to investigate.)

As Wikipedia's entry explains:

> Death metal vocals are often guttural roars, grunts, snarls, and low gurgles colloquially called death grunts or death growls....The lyrical themes of death metal often invoke slasher film–stylized violence, but may also extend to topics like Satanism, anti-religion, Occultism, mysticism, philosophy and social commentary....Although violence may be explored in various other genres as well, death metal elaborates on the details of extreme acts, including mutilation, dissection, torture, rape and necrophilia.[7]

Kind of makes you nostalgic for the Carpenters, doesn't it? "We've Only Just Begun."

A perceptive observer will notice a couple of themes emerging from the names of the bands that populate this icky corner of the musical world. Filling the iPods of America's angry young people are groups like Carcass, Entombed, Decapitated, Dismember, Pestilence, Sadist, Atheist, Suffocation, Asphyx, My Dying Bride, Disembowelment, Behemoth, Cynic, Napalm Death[8] ... I could go on, but you get the idea.

In our final stop on this tour of the music world's seedy underbelly of gore and blasphemy, allow me to cite a few of the (printable) song titles offered by a typical representative of these groups. Then we can all go take showers.

Recent albums by the group Autopsy have featured cheery tunes with titles such as "Twisted Mass of Burnt Decay," "Bonesaw," "Torn From the Womb," "Necrocanniblistic Vomitorium," "Tortured Moans of Agony," "Death Twitch," "Stillborn," and "Disembowel." Keep these little ditties in mind the next time you see a sullen "Goth" fifteen-year-old waiting at a school bus stop with earbuds in place.

I'm sorry I had to drag you through that sewer pipe. (Just be grateful I opted not to expose you to the lyrics of any of these songs.) But it is important to acknowledge the starkest forms of the national culture of death that is emerging around us—from the chi-chi, upscale art galleries in Soho, New York, to the seediest underground nightclubs of San Francisco. And the craze reaches beyond those trendsetting fringes.

The fact is, wherever we look in the realms of medicine, law, environmental policy, or diplomacy, we find misplaced priorities and twisted logic about life and death. And that upside-down thinking is driving policies with tragic results.

In this section I'll lay out a few examples for you.

11

VIRTUOUS ABORTION

FOR A SHORT time a few years ago Planned Parenthood's Web site would, for only fifteen dollars plus shipping and handling, sell you a T-shirt that declares, "I had an abortion." (Which, I suppose, gives new meaning to the phrase *dressed to kill*.)

The shirts were marketed right below the ever-tasteful "Choice on Earth" Christmas cards the group seems to push every December. Yes, nothing says Christmas cheer to your friends like a gentle reminder to defend partial birth abortion against regulation by those bloodthirsty, dangerous fringe groups . . . you know the ones . . . church members.

This misunderstanding about regular churchgoers was amplified when Hillary Clinton, in her role as secretary of state, said at a National Prayer Breakfast, "Yet across the world, we see organized religion standing in the way of faith, perverting love, undermining that message."[1]

If Planned Parenthood's Christmas cards co-opting the birth of the Savior to shill for the death of the unborn doesn't trigger your gag reflex, then the Mother's Day fund-raising e-mail they sent out in 2007 should do the trick. Yes, *Mother's Day.*

The e-mail was sent out in the name of actress Gwyneth Paltrow and her mom, actress Blythe Danner. In the e-mail the two explain that they "cannot stand idly by" while abortion "comes under attack" from pro-life groups and lawmakers.[2] After encouraging a generous donation to Planned Parenthood by Mother's Day, Paltrow and Danner offer this advice: "Tell your mom you've donated in her name. Or whisper it to your baby at bedtime."[3]

The mind boggles.

Of course you have to wonder if any of the women who responded to this appeal actually followed the "Danner-Paltrow Golden Girls'" suggestion.

Did some earnest young mother really make an online donation that would be used to "honor" her own mother and provide for the snuffing out of countless developing infant lives and then quietly slip into the nursery down the hall, push aside the plush toys, bend low over a cushioned bumper pad, nuzzle the peach-fuzzy little head, take in the amazing baby shampoo smell, hear the whistling little breaths, and whisper: "I did it in your name"?

You can only hope not.

Like the tone of the e-mail, the thought behind those "I had an abortion" T-shirts was to transform having had an abortion into something to be proud of rather than something to hide in shame.

Funny thing is, the shirts didn't sell all that well. In fact, a lot of pro-choice women were horrified by them. Planned Parenthood quickly pulled the shirts after a firestorm of protest generated mostly by friends and allies of the organization.

It seems no matter how often or how earnestly the abortion champions tell women that an abortion is just a medical procedure with all the moral implications of a tonsillectomy, the vast majority of women who have had one—and that's about one in every three women between the ages of fifteen and forty-five, by some estimates—still aren't buying it.[4] And that's clearly not because we pro-lifers have done such a wonderful job of influencing the culture.

It is because abortion pride is simply a very hard thing to sell to any woman who has gone on to carry a child to term later. After one spends nine amazing months tracking the growth of "the baby," listening for and hearing the heartbeat for the very first time, marveling at sonograms, praying and hoping that everything is OK, and weeping with wonder when you at long last hold that tiny, precious life in your arms—well, the tonsillectomy analogies tend to ring a little hollow.

At places like The Women's Clinic of Columbus, which I founded two years ago to provide an alternative to the abortion clinics in our city, we have surpassed the mark of our first one thousand babies saved from the abortionist's trade of death as a result of caring, compassionate staff and volunteers. We are determined to tell the truth in the face of a historic disinformation campaign and to rescue those who are scheduled for destruction. We are confident we can make a difference, one life at a time.

But if the pro-death crowd is anything, they are persistent in their misguided attempts to cause good people to call death a good thing.

As a matter fact, when it comes to Orwellian language twisting and gymnastic contortions of logic, you won't find a bunch more skilled at it than the passionate and tenacious advocates for abortion in this country.

Recently, National Public Radio (NPR)—a taxpayer-financed highbrow news and information network—decided that in its news operations, it would change the way it refers to activists on both side of the abortion issue. No longer would they talk about "pro-life" and "pro-choice" advocates. Instead, they'd refer to "abortion rights advocates" and "abortion rights opponents."[5]

So this is where we've come? On the most crucial moral issue of our time, a government-supported broadcast network can't admit that what we're talking about is the sanctity of human life?

It's incredible what some people will do to avoid the obvious—that a woman who is pregnant is carrying a baby and that an abortion takes the life of that baby.

Enter this strange realm and you find yourself in a place where developing baby boys and girls are instead called "the product of conception" or "fetal tissue." It's a place where a procedure that leaves women emotionally devastated and deeply soul-scarred is touted as a vital health benefit—despite the fact that it snuffs out a unique and irreplaceable human life, one that is desperately desired by the multitudes who are waiting in line to adopt.

Such language hijacking has been standard procedure for the coalition of radical feminists, population-control zealots, civil libertarians, and closet eugenics fans that make up the pro-choice movement. But recently they've begun to outdo themselves.

The "I had an abortion" T-shirt debacle was only one part of a larger strategy to sell America on the idea that having an abortion is actually a virtuous act—an admirable, even heroic step that should be applauded by all.

Enter *Ms.* magazine's "We Had Abortions" campaign[6]—a Web-based petition drive designed to coax as many as possible of the tens of millions of American women who have had abortions to, in essence, "Say it loud. I terminated and I'm proud!" When they delivered the petitions to President Bush and Congress, *Ms.* magazine press releases avoided saying how many signatures they had actually gathered—only that they numbered in the mere "thousands."[7] Once again the bandwagon seemed to be pretty sparsely populated.

In the same vein, the always-sensible California State Assembly passed a resolution encouraging us all to "celebrate" abortion and the *Roe v. Wade* decision. During the resolution debate, Republican assemblyman Tim Leslie clearly failed to catch the spirit of the celebration. Instead he publicly read the names of more than twenty women who had died from the so-called safe and legal abortions made available by the *Roe v. Wade* decision.[8] We pro-lifers sure know how to put a damper on a good party.

At a recent benefit banquet for our pro-life women's clinic, Eileen Smith, a passionate advocate for life, stunned us with her heartbreaking story of how her brilliant and beautiful nineteen-year-old daughter, Laura, left to visit her boyfriend and never came home.

Eileen received a phone call that Laura had died on an abortionist's table during a badly botched abortion. Later Eileen had the opportunity to ask two handwritten pages of questions of the man responsible for her daughter's death. "I found out later," she said, "that nearly everything he told me was a lie." At the conclusion of their meeting, Eileen told the doctor, "The blood of my daughter is on your hands; the blood of my grandchild is on your hands; the blood of every life you have ever taken is on your hands," and she went on from there. She said that he was silent with his head hung low.

This isn't to say that the abortion-pride campaign hasn't won over a good number of converts. Consider the Web site Girl-Mom, which describes its mission as providing support for Girl-Moms and affirming teens. Girl-Mom claims, "The only true crisis is the denial of the fact that teenage girls can be, are, and always have been, both sexual and maternal beings, with the capacity to love, procreate, and nurture."[9] A girl named "Kaya" posted a testimonial on the site under the headline, "I Chose Abortion and I'm Proud":

> I am proud that I made the best choice for my life and that of my child, even though the thousands of people who are yelling at women and trying to control their bodies try to make that choice look bad. I am proud I didn't let myself be bothered by the opinions of people who would ever judge another person for how they chose to control not only their bodies, but their future. I am proud that I stood up for myself and demanded a direction for my life that I wouldn't have been able to have, had I let myself be an incubator for a kid I had no desire in bringing into the world. I am proud that I focused on my own needs that were grounded in reality instead of the sentimental [expletive] surrounding a zygote or an embryo!...I [expletive] LOVE abortion, I tell other people all the time that I have had many of them, and would recommend the experience to anyone. No other experience in my life has liberated me so much. No other experience has challenged me so much, and not because it was emotionally hard, but because I had to stand up for myself and demand what I wanted in life and that is never easy. Rather than growing babies I have no interest in, I have grown and invested into my own life and future, and [expletives] yes, I am proud of that.[10]

I must tell you, my heart breaks when I read something like the above. In just a few sentences, Kaya echoed almost every insidious lie and rationalization the feminist/pro-abortion lobby has spewed for the past thirty-five years. In her words we hear the most destructive pathologies of our age: a stunning selfishness and self-absorption (count the occurrences of *I* and *my*) and a cold disregard for human life.

We also hear that twisting of language that goes hand in hand with living upside down. To Kaya, the child to whom she was being asked to *give life* was not a child who would be wanted and cherished by an adoptive family. No, she was being asked to be "an incubator for a kid" she didn't want. She viewed Western civilization's great tradition of holding human life precious as "sentimental [expletive] surrounding a zygote."

Here we have a glimpse into our society's dark future—if the forces who want to turn abortion into a virtue in the eyes of our culture have their way. It is a place in which most of us wouldn't want to live.

And in a culture where new life is so meaningless and *self* is so preeminent, not many people will—live, that is.

"MR. SMITH, YOUR ORDER OF STEM CELLS IS READY"

AMERICANS ARE PROBABLY more confused and misinformed about stem cell research than almost any other important topic. (A possible exception is the "infield fly rule" in baseball. In all honesty, I still don't get that one.)

It's not hard to understand why. Wade into the debate about stem cells, and you quickly encounter a lot of scientific jargon and conflicting opinion. You also encounter sincere people who are desperate to see themselves or a loved one cured of a horrible, fatal disease. You also find groups who stand to make billions if they can be the first to come up with such cures.

Put all that together, and you have a formula for disinformation—one stuffed with guile and wrapped in sentimentality—which, by the way, describes the flap over stem cell research that erupted during the 2006 election cycle.

Before revealing the unseemly truth about that ugly season and the even greater ugliness that has followed since, it is important that I make sure you understand two important distinctions: First, you need to know that there is a difference between *stem cell research* and *embryonic stem cell research*. The former involves stem cells that can be harvested in a number of nonlethal ways, such as from adult bone marrow and from the umbilical leftovers of live birth, to cite just two sources. The latter involves creating an actual human embryo (often a clone of a living person) and then destroying that embryo in order to harvest his or her stem cells.

This is a massively significant distinction that the advocates of embryonic stem cell research and their allies in the mainstream media consistently neglect to acknowledge. (This was just an accidental oversight, I'm sure.)

The second important distinction involves the difference between embryonic stem cell research and *federally funded* embryonic stem cell research. The former takes place with dollars from giant, multinational pharmaceutical companies, universities with huge endowments, and dead billionaires whose foundations offer grants. The latter is funded only after the government reaches into your wallet or purse.

It is no exaggeration to say that if more people had been offered a handle on these two sets of distinctions, the U.S. Senate and House almost certainly wouldn't have changed hands in 2006 (as I'll soon demonstrate), and actual grown-ups would have remained in charge, rather than Harry Reid, Nancy Pelosi, and company.

Over and over during that campaign season, the public was told that President Bush and his allies in Congress had banned stem cell research. The argument continued to say that if more enlightened, less spiteful people were in charge, miraculous cures for everything from Alzheimer's disease to spinal-injury paralysis would be rolling off the assembly lines in no time. Of course, none of it was true.

The Bush administration hadn't banned stem cell research at all. It had restricted *federal funding* of certain types of *embryonic* stem cell research. Do you see the difference? Clearly the media and a lot of celebrities didn't. Advocates fanned out across the country repeating the lies. Even the left-leaning political watchdog Web site Spinsanity.org observed the duplicity:

> In his response to President Bush's radio address on August 7, Democratic presidential nominee John Kerry drove home one talking point—that President Bush had banned embryonic stem cell research. He began by saying, "Three years ago, the President enacted a far-reaching ban on stem cell research," and later referred once to "the stem cell ban" and twice to "the ban on stem cell research." He

never clarified his use of the word, leaving listeners to believe that President Bush has banned all stem cell research. But that is simply not true.... Unfortunately, this is part of a pattern....[1]

Several weeks earlier, Ron Reagan, the son of the late President Ronald Reagan, had addressed the Democratic National Convention, and thus the nation, on the same subject. The speech was filled with wildly exaggerated claims; misleading appeals to emotion; and bad, old-fashioned falsehoods as Reagan Jr. invoked his father's suffering from Alzheimer's disease. As Ramesh Ponnuru noted:

> Ron Reagan began by saying he was "not here to make a political speech." (He just wandered into the convention hall and found himself in front of a TelePrompTer.) He was here, rather, to talk about "what may be the greatest medical breakthrough in our or in any lifetime: the use of embryonic stem cells—cells created using the material of our own bodies—to cure a wide range of fatal and debilitating illnesses: Parkinson's disease, multiple sclerosis, diabetes, lymphoma, spinal cord injuries, and much more. Millions are afflicted.... Now, we may be able to put an end to this suffering. We only need to try."[2]

You have to admit, it takes some truly breathtaking nerve to climb up on top of the mountain of goodwill and affection most Americans have for the memory of our most pro-life president and use it as a pulpit for advocating something that violates everything he ever stood for. It was shameful, but it was effective.

However, the ultimate low blow on behalf of the forces of embryo-destroying research was delivered by none other than actor Michael J. Fox.

I don't know a single person, myself included, who isn't saddened to see the popular actor's progressive deterioration as he battles Parkinson's disease. We have all been moved by his courage and positive attitude. It is also evident that Fox is a great dad, a devoted husband, and a genuinely decent human being. But when he put that enormous reservoir of support and sympathy into the service of influencing two tight Senate races in 2006—races in which federal funding for stem cell research was a central issue—he did us all a disservice.

Fox appeared in television spots aired on behalf of successful candidates Claire McCaskill in Missouri and Ben Cardin in Maryland. In the Cardin spot, Fox said:

> Stem cell research offers hope to millions of Americans with diseases like diabetes, Alzheimer's, and Parkinson's. But George Bush and Michael Steele would put limits on the most promising stem cell research. Fortunately, Marylanders have a chance to vote for Ben Cardin. Cardin fully supports life-saving stem cell research. It's why I support Ben Cardin. And with so much at stake, I respectfully ask you to do the same.[3]

I have great respect for the messenger, but I completely disagree with the message, because in it we find all of the typical deceptive half-truths and inflated promises.

Both McCaskill and Cardin won their races—and the Senate shifted to Democrat hands by a one-seat margin.

Across the country, the warnings from those of us who held deep concerns about embryonic stem cell research were buried in an avalanche of distortion and emotion such as that which saturated the Michael J. Fox political ads. I remember being told point blank by a nationally syndicated television host that researchers said embryonic stem cell research held great promise. Unfortunately, none of those promises have been fulfilled, and it is small consolation that the months since then have validated virtually everything we tried to say.

- We said the wild claims for embryo-destroying research were unfounded. That has indeed been the outcome.[4]

- We said that there were more promising alternatives on the horizon, utilizing adult stem cells. That too has proven to be the case.[5]

- And we warned that ignoring the ethical and moral implications of creating human life for the express purpose of destroying it—even if for noble ends like curing disease— would put mankind on a slippery slope with a chilling endpoint. Sadly, that too has proven to be the case as a chilling example from Ukraine, below, shows.

A news item from the BBC provides a peek at our Brave-New-World future:

> Healthy newborn babies may have been killed in Ukraine to feed a flourishing international trade in stem cells, evidence obtained by the BBC suggests. Disturbing video footage of post-mortem examinations on dismembered tiny bodies raises serious questions about what happened to them. Ukraine has become the self-styled stem cell capital of the world. There is a trade in stem cells from aborted foetuses, amid unproven claims they can help fight many diseases. But now there are claims that stem cells are also being harvested from live babies.[6]

This is precisely what many of us warned about, and we were widely mocked and dismissed as cranks for our trouble. Of course, I'm not holding my breath for apologies, retractions, or even simple acknowledgments of the truth from Ron Reagan Jr. and the rest of the crowd that clamored so loudly and so self-righteously about all this. After all, being loudly and cleverly wrong bought them some political power. It worked!

For liberals and embryo destroyers, the ends always justify the means. And for those living upside down, activism means never having to say you're sorry.

IF THIS IS YOUR MERCY, I'D HATE TO SEE YOUR VENGEANCE

THE SCENE HAS played out countless times: a depressed, distraught individual stands out on the ledge of a tall building trying to work up the nerve to jump.

Historically we've believed it our basic human duty to try to talk the person down. We point out that things might look brighter tomorrow. "Come back inside and let's talk," we plead. "You may feel differently in a few days."

Usually they do. But in the age of the "right to die" and physician-assisted suicide, we're now told that the "compassionate" thing to do is not to talk these hurting souls down, but rather to place your hand firmly on their backs and give them a good shove.

As America's original "Dr. Death," Jack Kevorkian has said about ending the life of a terminally ill patient, "You are not ending their life. I didn't do it to end the life. I did it to end the suffering the patient is going through. The patient is obviously suffering."[1] He apparently feels it's his duty to end suffering, even if it means ending a person's life.

Determined people have always been able to take their own lives. As a civilized society, we have never considered it our duty to assist them in fulfilling that determination. But as debate about Oregon's assisted suicide law and the Terri Schiavo case both revealed, that may be changing.

Poor Terri Schiavo. By the time the woman died—roughly two weeks after her feeding and hydrating tube had been disconnected by court order—many Americans were so weary of hearing wall-to-wall coverage and debate of the tragic and complex case that many were asking to be put out of their own misery.

Their weariness with it all was understandable. The Schiavo case was gut-wrenching. On the one side stood the woman's husband and dozens of pro-euthanasia groups; on the other were her parents and a host of pro-life groups. There were fourteen appeals and numerous motions, petitions, and hearings in the Florida courts; five suits in Federal District Court; Florida legislation struck down by the Supreme Court of Florida; a subpoena by a congressional committee to qualify Schiavo for witness protection; federal legislation; and four denials of *certiorari* from the Supreme Court of the United States. So, yes, the Schiavo-story fatigue was understandable, but it was also unfortunate.

Most Americans believe that, in the face of suffering and imminent death, it is legitimate for a patient and doctor to decide not to undertake further treatment. That is why people make out living wills and advance directives. Yet at the heart of the debate over physician-assisted suicide is a very different question: Should doctors not only *allow* death when it is imminent, but also *induce* it when a patient or his family requests it?

Over the years as a pastor, I have probably had the opportunity to be with more people who were facing death than others. I have seen first-hand the toll that suffering takes on not only the human body but also the soul. There have been occasions when death's embrace would seem to be a mercy. But for a medical doctor to take direct action to cause a patient's death seems to me to intrude into an area reserved for someone who sits far above mere mortals, regardless of what kind of training they have acquired.

In Ramesh Ponnuru's powerful book *The Party of Death: The Democrats, the Media, the Courts, and the Disregard for Human Life*, there is a chapter titled, "The Doctor Will Kill You Now."[2]

It is an apt title, because there is a world of difference between allowing death and proactively causing it. But that is precisely the distinction that was lost in the Terri Schiavo debate over physician-assisted suicide.

I must tell you, as a supposedly civilized culture, we need to think long and hard before we put our healers in the business of killing.

The American Medical Association's (AMA) code of ethics says physician-assisted suicide is "fundamentally incompatible with the physician's role as healer, would be difficult or impossible to control, and would pose serious societal risks."[3]

This practice, first approved in Oregon and now legalized in the states of Washington and Montana, doesn't just run counter to the AMA's code of ethics; it runs counter to common sense, human decency, and three thousand years of Judeo-Christian tradition.

A generation ago people trying to make the concept of euthanasia more palatable to the public promoted the euphemism *mercy killing*. Today the politically correct term is *physician aid in dying*. Whatever you call it, if advocates are successful in making it an accepted medical practice in this nation (as it already is in certain quarters of Europe), it is very possible that the "*right* to die" will eventually become "the *duty* to die."

Yale Kamisar, the Clarence Darrow Distinguished University Professor of Law Emeritus at the University of Michigan Law School, rightly asked, "Is this the kind of choice…that we want to offer a gravely ill person? Will we not sweep up, in the process, some who are not really tired of life, but think others are tired of them; some who do not really want to die, but who feel that they should not live on, because to do so when there looms the legal alternative of euthanasia is to do a selfish or cowardly act?"[4]

I remember Sunday mornings as a child in uncomfortable clothes sitting on a hard wooden pew. I also remember the hymns that helped to shape my worldview. Discussing this subject, I hear the choir singing "rescue the perishing, care for the dying."[5] But if physician-assisted suicide becomes accepted in America, the perishing and dying among us will surely face subtle pressures to avail themselves of the suicide option.

Surveys have shown that the groups in our society most concerned about the prospect of legalized, physician-assisted suicide are the elderly and the disabled. That should come as no surprise. They are the groups most likely to face pressure to get out of the way in an age in which the sanctity of life has been replaced by cold, "cost-benefit analysis" calculations.

What will happen if at some point the Supreme Court strikes down every state law against physician-assisted suicide? (This very nearly happened in 1998.) As an essay in *TIME* magazine stated, "You may want to live those last few remaining weeks or months. You may have no intention of shortening your life. But now the question...will be raised routinely: Others are letting go; others are giving way; should you not too?"[6]

Where death and dying are concerned, you can get a glimpse of America's future by looking at Holland. Physician-assisted suicide has been practiced there for almost three decades now. In a *TIME* magazine essay about Holland's experiment, Dr. Charles Krauthammer wrote:

> Indeed, legalization has resulted in so much abuse—not just psychological pressure but a shocking number of cases of out-and-out involuntary euthanasia, inconvenient and defenseless patients simply put to death without their consent....[7]

If America's next crop of Dr. Kevorkians gains the sanction of law, you can expect no better here and probably much worse. With some surveys showing more than 75 percent of Americans claiming to support legalization of physician-assisted suicide, we need to stop and ask ourselves a question: Who among us wants to grow old in the society we are on the verge of creating?

Psalm 41:1 says, "Blessed is he who has regard for the weak; the LORD delivers him in times of trouble" (NIV). How much regard for the weak will our society retain when physician-assisted suicide has long been the law of the land? How will we be viewed in the eyes of God when we measure people's quality of life to decide who deserves to live and who is a waste of resources? And can we expect deliverance in the time of trouble when the weak must justify their own existence?

As Kristi Hamrick has written:

A society that loses the sanctity of life has nothing left to share but death. If there are no reliable standards of right and wrong, then there is no reason to persevere or overcome, if you don't want to. No reason for people to reach out to you in your darkest moment if they don't feel like it. If we have no common dignity as humans, the only thing we share is a common end.[8]

Are we becoming a society in which you must justify your existence in order to be permitted to live?

In her now famous (or infamous, if you listen to the mainstream media) use of the term *death panels*, Sarah Palin rightly pointed out that several of the various Obama-Reid-Pelosi versions of health care reform that were considered for passage required hospital committees to handle "end of life" issues and provide guidance. Palin, as usual, was buried in an avalanche of outrage, mockery, and vilification for her statements. PolitiFact.com, the fact-checking Web site of the left-leaning *St. Petersburg Times*, voted Palin's assertion their 2009 "Lie of the Year."[9]

There is just one problem. As the Cato Institute and other think tanks pointed out (not that anyone in the mainstream media was paying attention), Palin was absolutely right. In their @Liberty blog site, Cato's Alan Reynolds authored a detailed analysis entitled, "Death Panels? Sarah Palin Was Right."[10] And Newt Gingrich came to her defense on George Stephanopoulos's Sunday morning program, *This Week*.[11] So did dozens of other knowledgeable folks who had actually bothered to read the monstrosity of a bill.

No less a left-leaning economist than the *New York Times* columnist Paul Krugman said on the ABC News program *This Week*, "The advisory panel which has the ability to make more or less binding judgments on saying this particular expensive treatment actually doesn't do any good medically and so we are not going to pay for it. That is actually going to save quite a lot of money. We don't know how much yet."[12]

As with the death panels controversy, all discussions of end-of-life issues invariably turn to the issue of "quality of life." The standard argument goes something like this: "When a person's quality of life drops to a certain level, it is justifiable and even laudable to end that person's life." But who makes that determination? Perhaps in the future, a government department will create a quality of life index. The sick, weak, and elderly whose quality of life quotient falls below a certain level could then be encouraged to stop using scarce resources and be assisted in dying.

In a world where that constitutes "mercy," what does vengeance look like?

TRAMPLE THE POOR, PRETEND
TO SAVE THE EARTH

ERE'S A PLOT synopsis for a movie script:

Some poor, struggling families who have suffered decades of extreme hardship and brutal oppression are finally about to get a chance for a better life. Amazingly, with that better life will come environmental renewal and restoration for the poisoned, polluted land in which they live. It is a near-miraculous outcome.

But just as these pitiful souls are about to enjoy the first positive developments of their lifetimes, one of the richest men in the world decides he doesn't like what's going on there. He pulls together some of his billionaire buddies and starts using their enormous power and influence to put a stop to the poor folks' miracle.

In spite of the overwhelming odds, the people put up a valiant struggle to keep alive the initiative that will end their misery.

Hollywood would usually snap up this story in a heartbeat. It has everything the moguls love—a David versus Goliath scenario and a rich, corporate fat cat for a villain. All it needs is a happy ending.

I'm saddened to have to tell you that this story did not spring from a screenwriter's imagination. It is a tragically under-reported news story with no happy ending. And the billionaire villain? It is the outspoken liberal George Soros, the benefactor of numerous Far Left organizations like MoveOn.org.

Although you almost certainly haven't heard about it, there is a community in the mountains of western Romania where mining has been going on for at least two thousand years. In fact, the Romans had a mining operation in Roşia Montana back when the apostle John was on the Isle of Patmos.

There is literally "gold in them thar hills." But two millennia of crude mining—especially decades of careless exploitation under Communist dictatorships—have left countless mountains of rubble that continually leach toxic chemicals into local streams and water supplies.

Geologist and author Paul Driessen describes the current plight of the local people this way:

> When the Ceaucescu government collapsed, state-run mines like Rosia's limped along, posting huge losses and continuing to ignore their environmental impacts. In 2006, most were finally shut down. Thousands of workers lost their jobs, villages were plunged into poverty, and families were reduced to surviving on pitiful welfare payments, scavenging for mushrooms and berries in the forests, and breaking up abandoned concrete facilities with hammers, to recover and sell their steel reinforcing rods. Few families own a car. Indoor plumbing is almost unknown. Snowstorms make unpaved roads treacherous, and malnutrition and ill health are common.[1]

Into this bleak and desperate picture stepped the Canadian mining company Gabriel Resources, with a classic win-win-win proposition. They proposed to reopen the mines using the latest, environmentally responsible methods *and* clean up the toxic nightmare left behind by the former Communist regimes—delivering a huge economic boost to a desperate population in the process. The proposal would create thousands of jobs. Gabriel Resources's proposal also included a plan to build homes and preserve deteriorating ancient churches.[2]

Driessen—a senior policy advisor for the Congress of Racial Equality—estimates that the plan would "... inject US $2.5 billion into the Romanian economy. The region would also get improved roads, wireless internet service, safe running water, modern schools and clinics, and dozens of new businesses—all of which would remain long after the mines finally close for good."[3]

So who could possibly oppose such an elegant solution for lifting suffering people out of poverty?

The global anti-mining movement, populated and financed by hyper-wealthy elites in America and Europe—that's who. Chief among them are George Soros and his Open Society Foundation and San Francisco gazillionaire Richard Goldman.

The Gabriel Resources project was an irresistible target because it violated the dominant upside-down thinking of our day on several counts.

First, mining is all about humans benefiting from and utilizing resources found in the earth. And as we've seen repeatedly in this section, a common theme is that humanity is *always* the bad guy. Almost any use of the earth's resources to benefit mankind is suspect from the get-go. And it's easy to scare the uninformed about mining because it has indeed been so environmentally destructive in the past. Plus, modern gold mining methods do utilize the compound cyanide—which everyone recognizes as a poison (especially readers of Agatha Christie mystery novels).

What "greens" such as the Soros-backed organizations conveniently fail to mention in this debate is that Gabriel Resources has developed a remarkable "closed loop" system for processing ore, which prevents any of the chemicals being used from entering the ecosystem.

But, no, the "greens" just need to run up and down the street yelling, "They're going to use cyanide!" to get government regulators and neighboring nations spooked.

While trying to frighten people about the prospects of a massively unlikely environmental problem if the Gabriel plan were to go forward, they ignored the fact that an honest-to-goodness environmental catastrophe would most surely continue if environmentalists proved successful in killing the project. Ironic, huh?

Secondly, most "greens"—zealous, socialist-leaning environmental true believers—despise market-oriented solutions like the one proposed by Gabriel Resources. (Someone jokingly labeled these types of environmentalists "watermelons"—green on the outside, red on the inside.[4])

In true Will Rogers fashion, they never met a government-mandated program they didn't like or a corporate initiative they didn't hate. This, in spite of the fact that top-down government approaches are usually inefficient and often counterproductive.

Let someone offer a solution to poverty and environmental distress that doesn't transfer more power to a central government somewhere? That's an outrage. Propose one in which a private corporation stands to make some money in the process? Well, that's enough to send them over the edge.

And over the edge they went, with truckloads of foundation money to spend on what Paul Driessen called an "intense campaign of lies and vilification to stop the project."[5] Soros and friends marshaled an army of lobbyists, lawyers, and public relations types and even flew in professional agitators from other countries—the usual suspects who can always be counted on to show up and display outrage against whatever the Left's *target du jour* might be.

A gullible and complicit media faithfully reported as fact whatever the anti-mining pressure machine said about the situation. By Christmas 2007, that machine's efforts were paying off. The project was put on hold by the Romanian government. Hundreds of workers had been laid off. Thousands of others realized their prospects for employment were fading.

As Paul Driessen put it, "The Soros-Goldman Brigade is filled with holiday cheer. It's just sent Season's Greetings to some of the poorest people in all of Europe: 'May you freeze in the dark.'"[6]

The people of Roşia Montana were devastated.

> "They are laughing in our faces, while we are crying. They are happy for our sorrow," Marinela Bar said bitterly. "The so-called ecologists care only about themselves, not about the local community," Calin Cioara added. "They only mock people."
>
> "We have no words to express our disappointment. The company was our only chance for development. We are hopeless now," Daniel Pacurar said softly, echoing the despondency that has crept into the valley, despite Gabriel's determination to continue seeking the needed permits and move forward.
>
> "We'll spend the holidays together at the community center," Miorita Botariu said. "We'll sing carols and laugh together, maybe

for the last time. With the project, we could have been a happy, united community. Now we will lose our friends, our neighbors, our relatives, because everyone will try to live a better life—somewhere else."[7]

It has always amazed me that some people profess unbounded love for Mother Earth, while at the same time displaying unbridled contempt for our brothers and sisters who inhabit the rest of the planet. John the Baptist said that if we had two coats, we should give one to him who has none, and likewise with food.[8] Some people are just not content unless they have taken away from those who have little or nothing even the little that remains to them—including the hope for a better life.

Of course, I don't believe for a moment that the *goal* of these environmentalists was to keep these people poor. Yet it clearly didn't matter, because that was the primary effect. "Mother Earth" is the priority. Humans and their stubborn attachment to living are consistently viewed as part of the problem.

For most of the last eighty or so years, social liberals have proclaimed themselves the champions of the poor and oppressed. In fairness, there have been many whose compassion actually translated into a willingness to get their hands dirty and meet hurting people where they are.

But there is a growing and powerful brand of "progressive" that views humans always and only as a problem. Think I'm exaggerating? Take a look at a list of organizations and initiatives receiving millions of dollars from the Richard and Rhoda Goldman Fund—one of the deep-pocketed organizations in favor of killing the Gabriel Resources project—and you'll find a long list of population control and family planning groups scattered around the world. Here is just a partial listing and description of Goldman Fund grants handed out in 2007, with descriptions taken verbatim from the foundation's Web site:[9]

- Center for Reproductive Rights—Domestic Legal Program: to use legal strategies to advance reproductive freedom in the United States—$250,000

- Choice USA—Mobilize and train the future leaders of the reproductive choice movement—$100,000

- Feminist Majority Foundation—Campaign to Expose Fake Clinics: to develop and conduct a research and action campaign to educate the public about the disingenuous tactics of crisis pregnancy centers—$600,000

- Americans for UNFPA—One Woman Can: advocacy campaign to mobilize supporters for restored U.S. funding to the United Nations Population Fund—$125,000

- Ibis Reproductive Health—Middle East and North Africa Program: to expand knowledge of and access to reproductive health, services, and information through research and development of educational materials—$175,000

- Ipas—MVA Distribution and Training: to promote access to comprehensive, safe, and legal abortion care throughout the world—$500,000

- Izaak Walton League of America—Sustainability Education Project: to educate its members and policymakers about the link between population and habitat to build support for increased U.S. funding of international family planning programs—$60,000

- Center for Health and Gender Equity—U.S. Global Initiative for Comprehensive Sexual and Reproductive Health and Rights: to advocate for U.S. global funding and policies that ensure a comprehensive approach to sexual and reproductive health and rights—$300,000

The list goes on and on and on, with multiplied millions of grant dollars being poured into organizations, all with a single aim—to keep additional humans from being born on the earth.[10]

Meanwhile, the poor humans who have the misfortune of living in the Roșia Montana area of western Romania, after fifty years of being victimized by Soviet-style Communism, have now been mugged by American-style upside-down thinking.

"The cold is killing us," says Mircea Silaghi. "There is no public transportation. Our wood stoves barely keep us from freezing. We are living only a little better than in the Middle Ages."[11]

"Mission accomplished," the environmentalists would say. Maybe now, with hope destroyed, they'll stop burning up all the wood to stay alive, do the right thing, and give the dust of their bodies in death as a sacrifice back to Mother Earth.

SILENT SUMMER

AFTER SIXTY SECONDS on the Web page, the number on the clock-counter quickly rises to around eight hundred and continues to climb at a dizzying rate. It is jarring to learn that the ever-climbing tally represents the number of people in the world who have contracted malaria since you loaded the Web page. After a little more than two minutes on the site, the counter is headed toward two thousand.

A little to the right on the Web page, you see another counter; it has climbed to ten. That, you learn, is the number of people (mostly children) who have died in the one hundred twenty seconds since you began viewing the page. The number continues to eleven...then twelve.

The numbers tick up relentlessly and without remorse.

It is called the Malaria Clock page, and it is provided by JunkScience .com—an Internet site dedicated to debunking pseudo-scientific claims and exposing misuses of science. The group's research indicates that about 96 million people have died needlessly of malaria in the thirty-five-plus years since a popular book triggered a ban on the chemical that had been man's best weapon against one of the world's most deadly scourges.

The 1962 book was Rachel Carson's *Silent Spring*, an indictment of the use of pesticides, particularly DDT. Many consider Carson's book to be the founding document of the modern environmental movement. The title of the book flowed from the claim that the widespread use of DDT caused the shells of songbirds' eggs to become thinner and more fragile. Carson warned of a near future without the sweet sound of songbirds.

To be fair, there is good reason to believe that the *agricultural* use of such pesticides was excessive and somewhat indiscriminant at the time.

Yet Carson's book painted a picture so dire that overreaction and over-reaching were almost inevitable responses. The best seller and the media coverage that followed were so effective in turning DDT into a "scare word" that the initials carry grim and even sinister connotations to this day. As a *New York Times* article pointed out, "Ask Americans over 40 to name the most dangerous chemical they know, and chances are that they will say DDT."[1]

Do you want to hear something truly grim? Let's jump back a few decades and recall what much of the world faced before the development of DDT.

For centuries and right up through the 1950s, malaria was arguably the leading disease-based killer of human beings on the planet. One scientific paper estimated that malaria killed three million people each year in the first half of the twentieth century.[2]

Then the near-miracle of DDT came along. The *New York Times* article noted:

> A malaria-eradication campaign with DDT began nearly worldwide in the 1950s. When it started, India was losing 800,000 people every year to malaria. By the late 1960s, deaths in India were approaching zero. In Sri Lanka, then called Ceylon, 2.8 million cases of malaria per year fell to 17. In 1970, the National Academy of Sciences wrote in a report that "to only a few chemicals does man owe as great a debt as to DDT" and credited the insecticide, perhaps with some exaggeration, with saving half a billion lives.[3]

Where DDT was used (simply by spraying a very small amount on the walls of homes twice each year) malaria practically disappeared. DDT was and is nontoxic to humans, animals, and fish, especially in the small amounts used in malaria control.

But even during the period of these initial successes, some voices were critical of the programs. Why would anyone oppose an effort that was safe, effective, and saving millions and millions of children's lives? Well, that was just it. As an article in *21st Century Science & Technology* magazine explained:

Why was DDT banned, 30 years after its World War II introduction and spectacular success in saving lives? The reason was stated bluntly by Alexander King, founder of the Malthusian Club of Rome, who wrote in a biographical essay in 1990, "My chief quarrel with DDT in hindsight is that it has greatly added to the population problem." King was particularly concerned that DDT had dramatically cut the death rates in the developing sector, and thus increased population growth.[4]

There you have it once again—the common thread of upside-down thinking that appears in every chapter in this section. It is thinking in which human life is cheap at best and an undesirable problem to be eliminated at worst.

What gave an opening to those like Rachel Carson who wanted to see DDT use banned was the fact that, in the United States, DDT was eventually used for more than malaria control; it was sprayed on cotton fields and used as a general measure of agricultural insect control.

Along came the national *Silent Spring* phenomenon beginning in 1962, even though numerous experts argued that the book contained inaccuracies and distortions.[5] By 1972, DDT had become so demonized and public outcry so strong that in April of that year, the Environmental Protection Agency (EPA) convened hearings on the matter. After seven months of testimony, EPA Hearings Judge Edmund Sweeney wrote in his decision that "[t]he uses of DDT under the regulations involved here do not have a deleterious effect on freshwater fish, estuarine organisms, wild birds, or other wildlife.... The evidence in this proceeding supports the conclusion that there is a present need for the essential uses of DDT."[6]

But two months later the Nixon administration's EPA head, William Ruckelshaus, a man with close ties to the Environmental Defense Fund, overturned Judge Sweeney's decision. Even though Ruckelshaus never attended a single day's session in the seven months of EPA hearings, and later admitted he had not even read the transcript of the hearings, he confidently asserted that DDT was a "'potential human carcinogen' and banned it for virtually all uses."[7]

This isn't the first time a government official made a critical decision without being encumbered by the facts. In March 2010, House Speaker Nancy Pelosi, referring to the behemoth health care bill that was being rammed through Congress, said, "But we have to pass the bill so that you can find out what is in it..."[8] As the vote on the measure neared, it became obvious that many of our elected representatives had no idea what was in it either.

The ban on DDT had legal, economic, and psychological domino effects that reached to every corner of the world. Thirty-five years later, the bad old days are back.

I have been to the jungles of Guatemala, where I have seen children who have to sleep without the benefit of mosquito netting and who are at risk for their lives because of diseases borne by biting insects. Even for those who are fortunate enough to have a net around their beds, one tiny tear in that covering can cause a lifetime of suffering or a premature and unnecessary end to a life filled with promise.

Only AIDS now kills more people in Africa than malaria does. One in twenty children dies of the unnecessary disease there.[9] Many of those who manage to survive malaria suffer residual brain damage. As journalist Tina Rosenberg describes it:

> Each year, 300 to 500 million people worldwide get malaria. During the rainy season in some parts of Africa, entire villages of people lie in bed, shivering with fever, too weak to stand or eat. Many spend a good part of the year incapacitated, which cripples African economies. A commission of the World Health Organization found that malaria alone shrinks the economy in countries where it is most endemic by 20 percent over 15 years.[10]

What compounds the tragedy of all this is that it is completely avoidable.

The same amount of DDT that was once sprayed on a thousand acres of cotton could protect every single man, woman, and child living in the malaria danger zones of Mozambique for a year—at a cost of about

$1.70 per person.[11] Alternatives to DDT cost as much as ten to twenty times more.

Where DDT is used, people live, and the quality of their lives improves. Nevertheless, a wide array of powerful groups and agencies exerts various forms of pressure to keep the lifesaver from being funded or used—all in the name of protecting Mother Earth. Of this irony, JunkScience.com wonders:

> How is it that *Gaia* can be painted an Earthmother nurture-figure whilst demanding an annual sacrifice of roughly two million, four hundred and thirty thousand infants, pending mothers and their untallied unborn? This is not ecology. This is not conservation. This is genocide.[12]

In spots across Africa, Asia, and Central and South America, there will be some "silent summers." They will be silent because too many of the consummate village noisemakers—children full of laughter, singing, shouting, and rambunctious play—are gone.

Malaria will have taken them. Yet, in a very real sense, they will be victims of more common plagues of our times—apathy and inverted priorities—upside-down thinking.

THE GLOBAL WAR
AGAINST BABY GIRLS

WITH 2007 DRAWING to a close, the former Pakistan Prime Minister Benazir Bhutto was assassinated as she campaigned in parliamentary elections. She was most likely murdered by agents of al Qaeda—the radical Islamic terror group that views a Westernized, educated female leader like Bhutto to be an absolute abomination.

Bhutto was a feminist icon—and rightly so. She blazed trails for women by becoming the first female prime minister of an Islamic country.

Yet Benazir Bhutto's tragic death and excellent life shine a bright light on two outrageous examples of twisted thinking on the part of American feminist activists: first, her death reminds us of the relative silence on the part of feminist organizations about the plight of women in Islamist nations.

It's not that groups like the National Organization for Women (NOW) can't be very, very aggressively vocal. When motivated, they can ratchet up the noise machine to deafening levels. When Don Imus made tasteless and disparaging remarks on his nationally syndicated radio show about the Rutgers University women's basketball team, the National Organization for Women issued an "Action Alert" and urged women to contact CBS and MSNBC demanding that Imus be dropped. With the feminists' clout added to the noise of the well-oiled Al Sharpton grievance machine, Imus was eventually fired.

Of course, that was nothing compared to the feminist histrionics and caterwauling triggered by the nominations of men like John Ashcroft and Tommy Thompson in the opening days of the George W. Bush administration.

Patricia Ireland, NOW's president at the time, called the effort to derail Ashcroft's confirmation as attorney general nothing less than a battle to prevent "the savaging of everything we've worked for" and "saving our rights and constitutional protections."[1] NOW warned that if Ashcroft were confirmed, women would have to put their dreams for "good jobs and equal pay; freedom from harassment, discrimination, hate crimes and other violence...on hold...."[2]

My goodness. John Ashcroft had some seriously malevolent plans for America.

In spite of a blizzard of NOW press releases, news conferences, protests, sit-ins, walk-outs, shout-downs, and hokey-pokey feminist shake-it-all-abouts, Ashcroft was confirmed by the Senate and served for four years. Somehow the women of America emerged from the other side of that long national nightmare with all of their dreams intact.

But that didn't keep NOW and other feminist organizations from confidently wailing "The sky is falling" when Samuel Alito was nominated to fill a Supreme Court vacancy.

One feminist Web site, The-goddess.org, warned:

> Stop Alito—Save American Democracy
> I know you're thinking that title is an exaggeration. It's more accurate than you might think. The confirmation of Samuel Alito would represent a fundamental change in American policy. So fundamental that we may not look much like America in a few years.[3]

Well, a few years have passed since Alito's confirmation, and I think most people would agree that Justice Alito has not transfigured the good old U.S. of A.

NOW named its grassroots campaign to derail the Alito nomination (I promise, I'm not making this up) "Enraged & Engaged." The Enraged & Engaged page on NOW's Web site asked women:

Are you Enraged? Get Engaged! We need you to defeat Alito.

Don't miss this one-time opportunity to be a part of this intensive campaign to protect women's rights. There is work to be done, both in Washington DC and throughout the country.... We're also encouraging activists to organize in their communities. We need you in Washington DC to staff our Defeat Alito headquarters. We'll help arrange local housing; just give us your time.[4]

The point is, when feminist activist organizations get exercised about an issue, they can be very aggressively vocal, organized, and focused about bringing public attention to it. But when it comes to the horrible and degrading things women around the world are subjected to in the name of Islam, feminists have a hard time working up any good old enragement or engagement.

In countries where Islamic Sharia is the law of the land, women's rights are violated with impunity. For example:

- Women are publicly beaten for violating Islamic dress codes.

- Victims of rape are imprisoned or put to death while the perpetrators frequently go free.

- Young girls are murdered by members of their own families in "honor killings" if they don't fully comply with their families' orders about whom to marry.

- Women are denied education, wealth, basic freedoms, and are generally treated like property.

My wife often quips that there needs to be a Christian Organization of Women, but COW would not be an appropriate acronym! Nonetheless, the equality of women and their value need to be recognized globally while invading all religions' boundaries. It's ludicrous to cry aloud for equal rights and ignore religious implications that state otherwise.

You would think feminist organizations would be focusing significant portions of their resources and energy on raising public awareness of these atrocities. Yet one whose thoughts were so logically inclined would be proved wrong.

It is a contradiction *Minneapolis Star-Tribune* columnist Katherine Kersten noted as she commented on a NOW campaign called "Love Your Body," an initiative launched to counter America's obsession with thinness and body image. Kersten observed:

> While NOW is indulging in this nonsense, women in some Muslim countries are denied basic human rights and live in fear of their lives. "Honor killings"—in which a woman is murdered by her own family—are a phenomenon across the Middle East, according to a recent *New York Times* article. The reasons? "Family honor can be tainted by a woman's desire to go study at a university or her use of a telephone," says the *Times*. Between 100 million and 140 million girls and women have undergone female genital mutilation, according to the World Health Organization. Why do so few American feminists seem to give a rip?[5]

You can understand Kersten's confusion as you wonder: can't America's *I-feel-bad-about-my-body* crisis wait until the *girls-having-acid-thrown-in-their-faces-for-refusing-to-wear-a-veil* issue is addressed?[6] I'm just asking.

Consider the case of the nineteen-year-old woman in Saudi Arabia who brought charges against seven men for gang rape. After punishments were handed down to the rapists, the judge sentenced the young woman herself to two hundred lashes and six months in prison for being alone in a car with a man who was not a relative of hers.[7]

On our university campuses, bastions of "progressive" feminist thought and practice, the hypocrisy is even worse. Harvey Mansfield, writing about how little our elite universities have learned since 9/11, observes:

> The feminists at Harvard seek to remove every vestige of patriarchy in America, but they have said almost nothing about the complete dismissal of women's rights by radical Islam. To do so would be to attack Islamic culture, and according to multiculturalism, every

culture is equal and none is evil. They forsake women in societies that repudiate women's rights and direct their complaints to societies that believe in women's rights. Of course it's easier to complain to someone who listens to you and doesn't immediately proceed to slit your throat. No sign of any rethinking of feminism has appeared in the universities where it flourishes.[8]

As always, if you want upside-down thinking, head to a major university and take a hard left at the *Women's Studies* sign.

To be fair, there have been a few exceptions to this pattern of feminist silence and neglect. The group Equality Now is not nearly as prominent as NOW or some of the other like-minded groups, but to their credit, they have made the plight of women's suffering a real focal point. Among other initiatives, the group has established the Adolescent Girls' Legal Defense Fund, the stated purpose of which is "to support and publicize strategically selected legal cases, diversified to represent the most common and significant human rights abuses of adolescent girls."[9]

Still, silence is the general rule among groups that claim to champion women's rights. And it is contradictions such as this that Benazir Bhutto's murder spotlighted. She was killed precisely because she was a woman who refused to stay in "her place."

The second shaft of light cast on feminist inconsistencies by Bhutto's life concerns the fact that, in life, she was a bit of an embarrassment to feminists.

Back in 1995, Bhutto addressed the United Nations (UN) Fourth World Conference on Women held in Beijing, China. Like most UN confabs, the meetings were supposed to be a ten-day orgy of America-bashing (largely underwritten by American taxpayers) and endless feminist hectoring about reproductive rights and access to abortion.

In the opening plenary session, Benazir Bhutto rose to speak. She told the attendees, including First Lady Hillary Clinton:

> To please her husband, a woman wants a son. To keep her husband from abandoning her, a woman wants a son. And, too often, when a woman expects a girl, she abets her husband in abandoning or

aborting that innocent, perfectly formed child. As we gather here today, the cries of the girl child reach out to us.[10]

Bhutto went on to challenge the delegates, saying:

> This conference need [*sic*] to chart a course that can create a climate where the girl child is as welcomed and valued as a boy child, that the girl child is considered as worthy as a boy child.[11]

Way to kill everyone's buzz, Benazir.

Few people know that Bhutto had strong pro-life convictions and had been one of the few prominent feminists willing to speak out against the practice of sex-selection abortions—a practice that almost always results in the prenatal killing of girls because of a cultural preference for boys. This practice has expanded massively in the years since Bhutto addressed that UN conference.

As ultrasound technology reaches even the poorest, least developed parts of the world, cultural preferences for boys fuel what amounts to a global war against baby girls. I firmly believe that ultrasound technology was developed to help save lives, not jeopardize them. When I hear reports that ultrasound images are used to determine whether or not a baby is "worth" keeping, it tempts me to want to turn back the clock to the days when expectant parents found out if their baby was a boy or a girl when he or she was born instead of long before.

A study published in the British medical journal *The Lancet* reported that, over the past twenty years, as many as ten million pre-born females may have been aborted in India by families desiring the birth of a male heir.[12]

Just how out of hand is this practice? When left to nature, there will, on average, be about 1,050 girls born for every 1,000 boys.[13] Yet, among second children in India, female births number 759 for every 1,000 boys.[14] The UN estimates that about 7,000 baby girls are aborted in India every day—simply because they are girls.[15]

Where is the feminist outrage? Apparently it's busy railing against our culture's obsession with skinny thighs and high cheekbones.

China's one-child policy has fueled its own version of this war on girls. "Official census data for the year 2000 showed a male-female gender gap of almost 17 percent, in some provinces rising as high as 30 percent."[16] And it's happening all over the world. "A report from 2005 found a worldwide gender imbalance of at least 200 million more males than females, caused by the abortion of baby girls."[17]

Of course, there is no way to enforce a ban on sex-selection abortions as long as other elective abortions remain legal. That is why this issue is so radioactive for feminist groups.

Thus, as my friend and fellow Ohioan Ken Blackwell notes:

> One of the most prominent forms of discrimination against girls exists even before they exit their mother's womb.... [Yet] the National Organization of [sic] Women and National Abortion Rights Action League have been quiet on the subject. Their Web sites yield no substantive discussion of the practice, which has resulted in millions of missing girls. Perhaps these organizations do not want to face the facts regarding abortion.... [G]roups such as NARAL and Planned Parenthood have yet to take up the cause.[18]

The conspicuous exception to this silence is the group Feminists for Life. This pro-life organization—their most visible spokeswoman being actress Patricia Heaton—has been consistently vocal and persuasive in championing the cause of unborn girls around the world. I say, "Good for them!"

Here is a truth that few of the conflicted, pro-abortion feminists dare to confront: Wherever Judeo-Christian ideas lie at the root of a culture, the status of women has risen and gender equality is the norm. Where women are little more than slaves, you'll find that Christians are a tiny, persecuted minority. Ponder that.

Likewise with Judaism. Even in the Middle East, where wives and daughters in many nations are treated worse than livestock, Israel is an oasis of equality and opportunity for women. As I observed in chapter 6, this is a key to understanding why Israel is so hated by its neighbors. It is an island of modernity in a sea of medievalism.

This is what so few movement feminists understand: the Christian influences in our country that they so despise, resent, and vilify are integral threads in the cultural fabric that made women's gains possible.

WHAT GENOCIDE?

A FTER YEARS OF silence, the arbiters of American compassion discovered Sudan. Their discovery was about two million lives and four million refugees late, but better late than never. On behalf of all of us who have been working to save lives and free slaves in southern Sudan for over a decade, I say, "Welcome to the fight."

Little by little, news blurb by news blurb, awareness of a colossal tragedy in Darfur, a region in western Sudan, seeped into the American consciousness. Hollywood celebrities began to take notice and lend their notoriety to the cause of putting the ongoing crisis onto the cluttered radar screens of average Americans. That's a good thing, because what is happening there is a horror almost beyond description.

Reports vary, but suffice to say that since February of 2003, when the current phase of the Sudan conflict began, no fewer than two hundred thousand people have died and nearly 2.5 million have been displaced.[1]

The roots of what is now being officially called "attempted genocide" are both racial and religious. Those doing most of the killing in Sudan are Arab Muslims. Those doing most of the dying are black Africans, many of them Christians.

As this tragedy has unfolded, the Islamic government's military forces and their proxies, the Arab "Janjaweed" militias, have conducted numerous campaigns of ethnic cleansing, barbarism, and the systematic use of rape as an instrument of war. In spite of an international arms embargo against the Sudanese government, their war-making ability continues to be equipped by—guess who—the Russians and the Chinese. (You would think those guys would want to be on the right side of a conflict every once in a while, just to change things up.)

Sudan's humanitarian affairs minister, Ahmed Haroun, and a Janjaweed militia leader known as Ali Kushayb were charged by the International Criminal Court with fifty-one counts of war crimes and crimes against humanity.[2] How bad is your regime when your humanitarian affairs minister is charged as a war criminal?

Clearly, what is happening there is tragic. But it actually pales in comparison to the holocaust that unfolded in southern Sudan for more than a decade—with much less awareness or concern.

Yes, while the good times rolled here in American in the 1990s, as the Clinton administration presided over the amazing Internet boom, a new radical Islamic regime in Sudan's capital in the Arab north, Khartoum, was working to impose Sharia law on the entire nation—by force if necessary. That included the largely black Christian majority in the south.

Way back in 1995, Paul H. Liben sounded a grim warning in the Christian journal *First Things*:

> Armed to the hilt by Iran, Iraq, China, and others, Khartoum declared a jihad against the south. The result has been the escalation of one of our century's greatest human tragedies. No southerner, it seems, has been exempt from its horrors. Women have been raped by the tens of thousands, their children torn from their arms and compelled to convert to Islam. Young men have been kidnapped and forced to fight against loved ones. Entire villages and towns have been burned to the ground, their people burned alive or taken into slavery.[3]

But as horrifying as all that was, worse news was to come. A British Christian human rights organization called Jubilee Campaign reported "mounting evidence of the crucifixion of the male populations of entire villages."[4]

Outside of Christian media outlets, little notice was taken of the religion-based genocide taking place in southern Sudan, even though the horror stories continued to accumulate as the decade of the nineties rolled by.

Sadly, it's not that surprising that America's liberal media establishment couldn't be bothered to sound a consistent alarm about thousands of Christians being crucified in a dusty corner of Africa. What *is* surprising is that America's civil rights grievance industry and its media allies hardly raised an eyebrow at a new, full-blown African slave trade emerging in the closing decade of the twentieth century!

For years black Christian leaders tried in vain to get the Reverend Jesse Jackson to condemn the slavery, rape, and murder going on in Sudan.[5] Perhaps there wasn't enough money in it. Maybe he was too busy laying guilt trips on liberal whites about the slavery that ended here one hundred fifty years ago to take notice of an active slave tragedy in our own day.

But the hypocrisy reached its zenith in the person of Louis Farrakhan, leader of the Nation of Islam—a religious cult that blends Islamic terminology with black nationalism.

Even after the true nature of what was going on in Sudan was widely known, Farrakhan maintained friendly ties with the radical Islamic government there. As the Anti-Defamation League reported in 1997:

> Despite mounting evidence pointing to the disturbing reality of Black enslavement in the Sudan, Minister Louis Farrakhan and the Nation of Islam maintain ties with Sudanese President Omar Hassan al-Bashir and leader of Sudan's ruling party, Hassan al-Turabi. Under this leadership, the country has become a base for Islamic extremist terrorism, and Muslim enslavement of Sudanese Blacks has persisted. The Minister refuses to condemn the current regime regarding this atrocity occurring in Africa to his fellow Blacks.[6]

More than a decade later, Farrakhan and the Nation of Islam are unrepentant and unchanged in their indifference to staggering suffering on the part of black Africans. On January 4, 2008, the Nation of Islam's official newspaper, *Final Call News*, published an editorial that basically asserted that all the hoopla about suffering in Sudan was really a plot to justify a U.S. invasion in order to seize Sudan's oil fields. It even accused the Congressional Black Caucus of being in on the scheme.[7]

Reverend Jackson's silence and Minister Farrakhan's confusion notwithstanding, it really isn't that hard to figure what the right response is here. More than ten years ago I mobilized a humanitarian organization called Bridge of Hope for just such a crisis as this.

With the help of many gracious, compassionate donors, we have provided almost 23 million meals and more than $17 million worth of medical supplies. We've delivered more than 51,000 blankets and more than 1,000 new tents, providing emergency shelter for returning refugee families. We've dug deep-water wells that provide entire communities with clean drinking water.

But what I'm most gratified to report is that over the last nine years, Bridge of Hope has been instrumental in helping free more than 32,400 Sudanese slaves, returning them to their rejoicing families and loved ones.

But still it continues. Staggering levels of suffering and injustice are ongoing as I write.

I am fully aware that there are millions of peace-loving Muslims who wouldn't think of harming their neighbor, but I also recognize that we still must come to terms with the radicalized segments of Islam that need to be confronted from without and corrected from within. It seems more than a little contradictory to me that some radical Muslims affirm they are following the dictates of a religion of peace while declaring war on all those who disagree with them.

STERILIZED FOR THE PLANET

S INCE THE 1960s we have heard a steady drumbeat from environmentalists about how bad for the earth we humans are.

For nearly five decades people have been consistently portrayed as a kind of viral blight on the planet—a scourge bringing nothing but environmental catastrophe and habitat destruction wherever they spread.

For even longer the assertion that overpopulation is a serious problem has been an article of absolute faith among environmentalists. *Faith* is the right word because they hold fast to this belief in the face of strong evidence to the contrary. As I pointed out in my book, *Culturally Incorrect: How Clashing Worldviews Affect Your Future*, "That it is a bad thing when human beings reproduce themselves has become a 'given' in [the postmodern] worldview."[1]

For example, a biologist for the National Park Service was quoted in the *Los Angeles Times* saying, "We have become a plague upon ourselves and upon the earth....Until such time as Homo sapiens should decide to rejoin nature, some of us can only hope for the right virus to come along."[2]

That's right. What the world needs is not love, sweet love but a pandemic that will kill billions of humans, say the gentle lovers of Mother Earth. Another Black Death would be great! Do you think I'm exaggerating?

In a letter to Jay W. Richards, an authority on Intelligent Design and coauthor of *The Privileged Planet*, William Burger, a curator at the Field Museum of Natural History in Chicago, wrote:

> One of the things missing in your book...is the devastation humans are currently imposing upon our planet. Still adding over seventy million new humans to the planet each year, the future

looks pretty bleak to me. Surely, the Black Death was one of the best things that ever happened to Europe: elevating the worth of human labor, reducing environmental degradation, and, rather promptly, producing the Renaissance. From where I sit, Planet Earth could use another major human pandemic, and pronto![3]

Charming, eh?

Regarding that letter, Dr. Richards wrote:

It is naive to continue acting as if this type of death wish is reserved for isolated crackpots. On the contrary, it is well on its way to being respectable opinion in some quarters—held by the well educated and the otherwise civilized—just as eugenics was respectable a century ago.[4]

Now we have an entire generation of adults in the West who have been raised on this steady diet of alarmist, antihuman propaganda. So it shouldn't come as a surprise to learn that many people are following the logic of these beliefs to their natural endpoint: that is, if every single human born is another parasitic insult to what, without humans, would be a peaceful paradise, then the only responsible thing to do is not have children.

Across the Western world, birthrates have fallen well below the replacement rate of 2.1 babies per woman. The birthrate of the United States hovers right at the replacement level, but only because of massive immigration (legal and illegal) from countries south of our border. In fact, without illegal immigration, our birthrate would be closer to the rapid-extinction levels currently seen in Europe.

Of course, if it is environmentally good to limit yourself to one child, how much better to have none at all? That's precisely the conclusion a growing number of upside-down thinking, earth-conscious folks are reaching.

A headline in the British newspaper *The Daily Mail* declared: "Meet the Women Who Won't Have Babies—Because They're Not Eco Friendly."[5] The article introduces us to Toni, who'd had an abortion for environmental reasons ten years earlier and subsequently took further measures to save the planet:

> At the age of 27 this young woman at the height of her reproductive years was sterilised to "protect the planet." Incredibly, instead of mourning the loss of a family that never was, her boyfriend (now husband) presented her with a congratulations card. While some might think it strange to celebrate the reversal of nature and denial of motherhood, Toni relishes her decision with an almost religious zeal. "Having children is selfish. It's all about maintaining your genetic line at the expense of the planet," says Toni, 35. "Every person who is born uses more food, more water, more land, more fossil fuels, more trees and produces more rubbish, more pollution, more greenhouse gases, and adds to the problem of overpopulation." While most parents view their children as the ultimate miracle of nature, Toni seems to see them as a sinister threat to the future.[6]

Toni is not alone. She is part of an entire generation that has heard nothing but environmental doom and gloom since birth and now unquestioningly accepts the premise that humans have no rightful place on the planet.

Of course, there is a bonus to adopting this brand of environmentalism. While you're being selfless and noble, you get to spend all your time and money on yourself. As Toni reveals in the article, "Ed and I married in September 2002, and have a much nicer lifestyle as a result of not having children. We love walking and hiking, and we often go away for weekends. Every year, we also take a nice holiday—we've just come back from South Africa."[7]

And she says those of us raising children are the ones being selfish? OK...got it.

What is taking place across most of Europe and in places like Russia and Japan is nothing short of cultural and demographic suicide. This is precisely what Canadian author and columnist Mark Steyn has been valiantly trying to point out for several years now to anyone who will listen. In an article in the *New Criterion* entitled, "It's the Demography, Stupid," Steyn wrote:

> There will be no environmental doomsday....For 30 years, we've had endless wake-up calls for things that aren't worth waking up for. But for the very real, remorseless shifts in our society—the ones truly jeopardizing our future—we're sound asleep. The world is changing dramatically right now and hysterical experts twitter about a hypothetical decrease in the Antarctic krill that might conceivably possibly happen so far down the road there are unlikely to be any Italian or Japanese enviro-worriers left alive to be devastated by it.[8]

Here is the good news. There is a powerful antidote to this catastrophic form of upside-down thinking. You'll find it in the Book of Genesis. There we find God handing mankind the keys to a brand-new world with instructions to "cultivate it and keep it" and to "be fruitful and multiply" in it.[9]

You see, we belong here. (I can't believe I'm living in a day in which I have to point this out!)

God gave us the earth to use, enjoy, and, yes, care for wisely. One of the first instructions He gave to our pristine parents, Adam and Eve, was to be fruitful and multiply. He didn't make a mistake when He gave them those instructions, and the world's population hasn't taken Him by surprise. I am convinced the resources necessary for all of us to not just survive but to thrive are already in place. It's up to us to figure out how to use what God has already given us. It's a concept called stewardship.

Furthermore, bringing life into this world, nurturing children, and rearing them to be productive people of character is one of the noblest and most self-sacrificial things any person can do. Our greatest responsibility, and one God takes very seriously, is to raise up a righteous seed.

Raising children is hard, expensive, and often heartbreaking work. But doing so is a well-founded vote of confidence in our culture and in mankind's unique place in the world. The French philosopher Jean-François Revel wrote: "Clearly, a civilization that feels guilty for everything it is and does will lack the energy and conviction to defend itself."[10]

He was right. But I would also suggest one thing such a society *will* find the conviction to do—and easily. That is to commit suicide—one environmentally sensitive step at a time.

SUMMARY (PART 2)

I OPENED THIS SECTION with a cheery little overview of death metal music and its multiple sub-genres. (An old-fashioned grindcore sing-along, anyone? No? Just growl along, then.) So, for balance I will close it with what constitutes as much of the complete opposite of that relentless, nihilistic celebration of hate as you can ever know.

You see, I have been an avid student of the Bible since the time I learned to read, and after all these years, I am still struck by the Scriptures' front-to-back message—*life*.

The centerpiece of the Garden of Eden was the tree of life. Later, one of God's first messages to His newly formed covenant people, the Israelites, was an encouragement to "choose life."[1] Jesus introduced Himself to a waiting, dying world as "the way, the truth, and the life."[2] He explained His mission in life-from-death terms: "The thief does not come except to steal, and to kill, and to destroy. I have come that they may have life, and that they may have it more abundantly."[3]

The fact is, the entire unified Bible narrative can be seen as a cosmic battle against death—and for life. On the pages of Scripture, death is unequivocally the enemy. It is the defeated adversary taunted in the familiar question: "O Death, where is your sting?"[4]

Perhaps that is why the Bible now seems so jarringly out of phase with what Peggy Noonan has called our current "culture of death." Of the Columbine High School killers Noonan wrote, "The boys who did the killing, the famous Trench Coat Mafia, inhaled too deep the ocean in which they swam."[5]

Indeed, as we've seen in the preceding chapters, those waters are broad and exceedingly deep. In many ways we are all swimming in a culture of death.

Hollywood has learned that the only sure thing for a profitable film is one that pushes the envelope of torture, death, and gore. These days nobody in the movie business loses money depicting sadism and carnage (Quentin Tarantino and his reprehensible *Grindhouse* flop being the notable but rare exception). A new term has been coined to describe the wildly popular horror movies like the endless *Saw* and *Hostel* series: *torture porn*. (It's popular, and it's playing in your neighborhood theater.) Popcorn, anyone?

Indeed, in most places, it is easier to generate a groundswell of public sympathy with a news report about neglected cows than over the appalling realities of partial birth abortion. And if you're looking for outrage, don't mention abortion mills—try puppy mills instead. That will jam the switchboards.

Certainly too many among us have been marinating too long in post-modern culture's twisted blend of narcissism and secularism—one that simultaneously trivializes the tragedy of death and the preciousness of life. It's a grim picture.

And yet…I see reasons for cautious hope all around me. As I travel around this nation, I see something inside even those most saturated in the toxic marinade of selfish cynicism. I see the recognition that there is something unique about this creature, the human—an inward knowing that in man, God has done something extraordinary.

Though frequently buried and dormant, that *knowing* rises to the surface from time to time. It was there in our collective shock on the morning of September 11, 2001, when the very first news reports told us there might be as many as thirty thousand people trapped in those burning towers. And it was there in our collective relief and rejoicing when, a few months later, nine miners were pulled from a flooded Pennsylvania coal mine after three days underground—bringing a welcome bit of good news to a shell-shocked, anthrax-antsy nation that really needed it.

The *knowing* is there when we shake our heads at the news report of a wriggling, crying baby left in a cold alley garbage bin. It is what stirs us when we hear distant reports of battlefield valor in which one person lays down his or her life to save many others.

Yes, we are surrounded by violence. Yes, there are many who rationalize killing in the name of fulfillment, happiness, or even convenience. But there is hope.

Peggy Noonan spoke eloquently of it:

> It occurs to me at the moment that a gun and a Bible have a few things in common. Both are small, black, have an immediate heft, and are dangerous—the first to life, the second to the culture of death...[6]

She's right. The Bible is a threat to the current culture of death. Wherever its light is allowed to shine, the grim shadows of death disperse. Oh, how our upside-down culture needs to look to that light as an ancient mariner looked to the shining brightness of the North Star for guidance on dark, dark nights.

PART 3

ADULTS ARE CHILDREN...CHILDREN ARE ADULTS

OVERVIEW

O NE OF MY daughter Ashton Blaire's favorite childhood movies was *Freaky Friday*—the story of a mother and daughter who switched identities.

Adults living in the bodies of children and children who suddenly find themselves living in the bodies of adults—it's a popular movie plot device that makes for interesting situations and lots of opportunities for comedy.

In 1988's *Big*, Tom Hanks played a twelve-year-old kid who made a wish to bypass all the uncertainty and awkwardness of adolescence and jump right into adulthood. He got his wish but found that he was not quite prepared to handle the pressures of work and the complexities of grown-up romance.

Twenty years later we're granting a lot of kids pretty much the same wish. As a culture we are enabling and even pressuring children to live like grown-ups, but in most, if not all, cases they're no better equipped to handle it than Tom Hanks's character was.

As *Orlando Sentinel* columnist Kate Santich wrote a while back:

> They worry about their hair and makeup and how they measure up to the images they see in advertising. They talk of becoming pediatric surgeons and do PowerPoint presentations on marine biology. Their toys are pricey, their cell phones busy, their social calendars

booked solid. All around them are pressures to dress sexy, talk sexy, be sexy. And they're not even teenagers yet.[1]

Joni and I were mortified one night when we stumbled across the TV show *Little Miss Perfect*, which sensationalizes tiny girls strutting on stage made up like Barbie dolls, teased hair, spray tans, fake nails, fake teeth, and a fake identity soon to come.

It's not just the pressures and prerogatives of adults that kids are taking on these days. Some are exhibiting the very worst pathologies too—such as rape.

In 2007, three Acworth, Georgia, boys were charged with the rape, kidnapping, and false imprisonment of an eleven-year-old girl. The boys were ages eight and nine.[2]

That wasn't an isolated case. Across the country, local prosecutors have to figure out whether eleven-, twelve-, and thirteen-year-olds who commit brutal rapes should be charged as children or adults.

Here's a thought: could it be that the appallingly easy access to hardcore pornography now made possible by the Internet (if not at home, then perhaps at a friend's house) might be related to this horrifying trend?

"Nah!" say the civil liberties types. They confidently assure us there is no linkage whatsoever between porn consumption and sexual violence. But keep in mind that these are the same folks who oppose profiling in airport security lines because there is supposedly no link between being a young, male Islamic radical and the increased risk of terrorism.

Next they'll try to tell us there is no connection between my waistline and how frequently I visit the Krispy Kreme doughnut shop when the "Hot Now" sign is illuminated.

While our nation's kids increasingly behave like adults, we're also seeing the other side of the coin—what some have described as the "infantilization" of adult America.

Ten years ago, half of America was inclined to wink at President Bill Clinton's trysts and infidelities with a "boys will be boys" kind of resignation. Since then it has grown more and more socially acceptable—even fashionable—for grown men and women to behave like juveniles. Across the vast wasteland of television, an adult character who behaves like a bona fide grown-up is getting harder and harder to find.

Just check out *The Real Housewives of Orange County* if you want to experience junior-high behaviors manifested in thirty-something housewives wearing their teenagers' clothes. This kind of reality programming is anything but real. If you doubt it, take a look at their promotional pictures compared to the folks you sit next to on the bus.

Adolescent, irresponsible adults and sexualized, over-scheduled, under-protected children make great fodder for Hollywood scriptwriters. But in real life, they are a prescription for cultural disintegration.

In the chapters of this section I'll point out the manifold ways our culture is enabling and encouraging these tragic role reversals. Is "tragic" too dramatic a description? Read on and decide for yourself.

20

MEN WILL BE BOYS

AS THE SMOKE cleared from the attack on Pearl Harbor at the end of 1941, they flooded armed services recruitment offices by the millions—young men eager to defend their nation. Farm boys from small, rural towns as well as the sons and grandsons of immigrants from big cities were all eager to test themselves against the rigors and dangers of war.

Few men wanted to be left at home while other guys stepped up to defend the nation's honor, including those who weren't actually "men" yet—those who had not yet reached eighteen, the legal age to enlist.

By the tens of thousands, boys lied in order to get around the age restriction—boys like Ray Jackson, who managed to get himself into the Marines at sixteen. Well into his eighties today, Jackson is the author of three books about his fellow underage soldiers, including *America's Youngest Warriors*.[1] In an interview with ABC News, Jackson said: "With the underage veterans there were three things that drove this. One was patriotism. One was poverty. And the third was adventure."[2]

Audie Murphy, the young man from Texas who ultimately became the most decorated American combat soldier of World War II, tried to enlist at seventeen but couldn't bring himself to lie about his age.

Like Murphy, many of the underage recruits were seventeen and simply too impatient to wait for their next birthday. But many were much younger. Gerry Barlow manned an antiaircraft gun on a Navy aircraft carrier at the ripe old age of fifteen. Leonard Anderson, another fifteen-year-old who was hungry for adventure, cut class and slipped into a Navy recruiting station. Six months later he found himself experiencing perhaps more adventure than he bargained for as he drove an amphibious landing craft onto a beach at some faraway place called Iwo Jima.[3]

Columnist James Lileks writes proudly and movingly about his father, who also fibbed his way into the Marines while scarcely old enough to shave:

> My father was part of the force that would have invaded the Japanese mainland. He volunteered for this. At the age of 15.... If there had been no Pearl Harbor, a North Dakota boy might not have felt the need to head to the seas.... But because there was a Pearl Harbor, there was this one thin farmer boy on a ship in the middle of the trackless ocean, knifing through the waves to the battle of the mainland. And if he'd been torn to bloody ribbons like half his friends, I wouldn't be here, and my amazing [daughter] Gnat slumbering in the other room wouldn't be here either.[4]

By some estimates, more than two hundred thousand underage men (and some women) successfully enlisted in the armed services during World War II. Clearly it was an era in which boys were eager to be considered men and to put aside the sandlot, the bicycle, and the comic book and slip into the shoes their fathers wore.

In our upside-down day, it only seems appropriate that we have found a way to turn that phenomenon on its head. We have a culture in which many grown men want to dress, act, play, and even think like adolescents.

The apostle Paul once wrote: "When I became a man, I put away childish things."[5] But the old preacher from Tarsus would have been badly out of step with our times. Today we say, "When I started earning more money, I upgraded my game console and joined a paint-ball league."

In an age where youth is deified, teenagers rule, and the most highly coveted marketing segment consists of eighteen- to twenty-five-year-olds, it's getting harder and harder to separate the men from the boys.

This is a troubling trend to which Diana West devoted an entire book entitled *The Death of the Grown-Up: How America's Arrested Development*

Is Bringing Down Western Civilization. In it she cites some telling statistical trends:

> More adults, ages eighteen to forty-nine, watch the Cartoon Network than watch CNN. Readers as old as twenty-five are buying "young adult" fiction written expressly for teens. The average video gamester was eighteen in 1990; now he's going on thirty. And no wonder: The National Academy of Sciences has, in 2002, redefined adolescence as the period extending from the onset of puberty, around twelve, to age thirty.[6]

At the risk of sounding like Mr. Geezer McFogey, I have to tell you that when I see a thirty-five-year-old man walk into a nice restaurant wearing a backward baseball cap, a sports team jersey, and ripped jeans that appear to be in imminent danger of dropping to his ankles, a part of me wants to cuff that hat off of his head and shout, "What's wrong with you, man! You're *not* seventeen. You look ridiculous—and your son wants his clothes back!"

Don't get me wrong. I'm not suggesting that every guy on his twenty-first birthday should be fitted for a fedora and wingtips. Nor is the core problem the fact that an appalling number of American men refuse to dress like grown-ups. The trend that is really eroding our strength as a culture is that men increasingly refuse the *responsibilities* of adulthood.

At the age of twenty I was pastoring one of the fastest-growing churches in the nation, which I founded at the ripe old age of nineteen with seventeen people attending the first service. Before I was thirty years of age I was overseeing the completion of the largest sanctuary complex in three states. Perhaps I'm an anomaly in my generation, but I really don't think so. I do think our attention has been arrested by those who are making the most noise about how disadvantaged and disenfranchised they are. We tend not to notice those who are quietly going about the business of making their lives and the lives of those around them better by accepting their responsibilities.

The most fundamental of those responsibilities is standing on your own two sneaker-wearing feet.

For example, a startling number of older baby boomers are finding their dreams and hopes for their "empty nest" years complicated by one little factor—their nests refuse to empty. More and more fully grown single adults are living with their parents.

Some of this is obviously driven by the fact that, with soaring educational costs, greater numbers of young adults graduate with crushing loads of debt in the form of college loans. Others find themselves priced out of the housing market in coastal cities with disproportionate housing costs.

But a lot of these "boomerang kids," as they have been labeled (you throw them out and they just keep coming back!), either moved back home or never left in the first place simply because it is so much easier (and more fun) *not* to have to deal with all the responsibility of living on their own.

Census figures show that men are more likely to move back home than women. In fact, those figures revealed that 56 percent of all young men between the ages of eighteen and twenty-four were living with their parents.[7]

This epidemic of what sociologists have clinically labeled "extended adolescence" has unleashed a horde of oversized, oversexed juveniles with lots of spending money and no one in their lives to tell them no.

As you might expect, these guys break down in three groups according to whether they want:

1. Sex without marriage
2. Marriage without children
3. Children without real commitment to the family

In an article titled "Enabling Adult Immaturity," sociologist Mike Males, a senior researcher for the Center on Juvenile and Criminal Justice, wrote: "The deterioration in middle-aged adult behavior has driven virtually every major American social problem over the past 25 years."[8]

I would add that it has also fueled the rise of entire industries and entertainment empires built of feeding this demographic group's insatiable appetite for the jiggly and the juvenile.

A prime example is a program that called itself *The Man Show*. Now canceled but still seen in repeats, it was actually a thirteen-year-old's fantasy come to life. The show's basic elements were apparently beer, pranks, lewd-ity, crude-ity, and semi-nudity.

If that is *The Man Show*, some of us are operating with a different definition of a real *man*. But it is just one of scores of vehicles all scratching the same itch and trading on the same men-will-be-boys shtick. From MTV's *Jackass* where thirty-something-year-old guys do their best to live *down* to the name of the program, to Comedy Central's *South Park*, to just about any of the Cartoon Network's popular Adult Swim offerings—there seems to be no bottom to the American male's appetite for breasts (real or cosmetic), bodily function jokes, and blasphemy.

Of course, to find the fullest manifestation of this culture-killing train wreck in motion you have to enter the septic tank waters of digital satellite radio (XM and Sirius), which have become an uncensored, unregulated haven for shock jocks like Howard Stern and Opie and Anthony.

Preening. Petulant. Profane. Prurient. Pleasure-seeking. Pompous. Pampered. Porn-addicted.

This, my friend, is what passes for manhood in our day. I'm just grateful John Wayne isn't around to see the pitiful big-screen replacements currently portraying the iconic American male archetype.

A few years ago an extraordinary movement was launched in this nation with the goal of seeing men restored to something stronger... nobler...freer. It was called the Promise Keepers movement, and like an August prairie grassfire, it swept the nation. In city after city men filled stadiums and made solemn personal vows to God and to self—vows that were all about being better husbands, fathers, friends, citizens. In other words—about being better *men*.

Predictably this movement was attacked by the Left and mocked by the popular culture.

Feminist groups—ignoring facts, evidence, and common sense, as usual—accused Promise Keepers of being all about husbands dominating their submissive wives. Right. You bet. Having a husband that pledges to be faithful to her, abstain from pornography, and be more involved in rearing the children. That's every wife's nightmare, all right. Thanks, NOW, for your bold advocacy for women.

In addition to being attacked by the feminists, the movement was attacked by the *effeminate*. An article in *GQ* magazine—that bastion of all things manly—compared the group's stadium events to Nazi rallies.

How upside down is that?

In the 1940s we had boys who did everything they could to pass for men. Today we have men who strive to pass for boys. We've gone from Audie Murphy to Howard Stern in three short, misguided generations.

BIG MOTHER IS LISTENING

Now Mark, we don't say things that hurt others people's feelings, do we? You apologize right now or else."

"Ezra, the pictures you drew made some people sad. I'm afraid we're going to have to take away your paper and ink. No remorse? Then you're headed for a time out, young man!"

It's not unusual for a mom to take swift action when children say or do things others find offensive. In a previous era, inappropriate words might get a kid's mouth washed out with soap. The fact is, good parenting has always involved making sure toddlers and preschoolers learn to mind their manners.

But what if the people being punished for their words are journalists? And what if it is the powerful might of a national government that decides to play the role of "Mother"? And what if punishment is handed down for simply being seen as rude by some easily offended party? And what if the punishment is severe enough to ruin a good man?

As bizarre as it sounds, it is precisely what some good men in Canada are facing. And it is something the powerful forces of political correctness hope to bring to the United States in the very near future.

You may recall that the all-powerful government in George Orwell's *1984* created the concept of "thought crime" and warned citizens to stay in line with the saying "Big Brother is watching." Well, something chillingly similar is emerging north of our border, but with this kinder, gentler form of thought-policing, it might be more appropriate to say, "Big *Mother* is listening."

The delicious irony of it all is that those delicate Canadian flowers that have been so deeply offended by a few words and pictures are part of the greatest force for repression and intolerance currently at large on Planet Earth.

Allow me to explain.

Remember those Danish cartoons that got the imams and ayatollahs so worked up a few years ago? They were published in several countries as a deliberate test of Europe's commitment to freedom of the press in the face of a growing Islamic immigrant population—a population that had been showing tendencies to bully Western governments into curbing freedoms and gradually adopting Islamic Sharia law.

At first those cartoons went largely unnoticed. Then a few Islamic agitators went on a tour of the Middle East with the intent of whipping up a foamy, frothy head of outrage among the faithful. With the help of some ultra-offensive cartoons that hadn't actually been published, they succeeded. The usual riots, looting, mayhem, and murder ensued. Whole nations declared boycotts of Denmark and other European nations.

In other words, it was a big, big news story.

And what do credible news magazines and newspapers in a Western democracy do with a big, big news story? Why they report it, of course. In detail—even if some interested parties wish they wouldn't. It's not only their right to do so, but it's also their duty.

That is what Ezra Levant, publisher of the *Western Standard* magazine, did. It eventually landed him in hot water with an agency in Canada called the Human Rights Commission (HRC). The complaint to the HRC was initially lodged by a radical Muslim imam named Syed Soharwardy. It was later joined by other members of what seems to be a rapidly growing Muslim grievance club—a fraternal order of whiners with astonishingly tender feelings and delicate sensibilities. This is despite the fact that they tend to hold opinions that many women, Jews, gays, and Christians most certainly find offensive.

In an essay published in the newspaper the *Globe and Mail*, Levant described his first interrogation by Human Rights Officer Shirlene McGovern:

I was there because I was compelled to be there by the government, and if I answered Officer McGovern's political questions unsatisfactorily, the government could fine me thousands of dollars and order me to publicly apologize for holding the wrong views.

I told her that the complaint process itself was a punishment. Even if I was eventually acquitted, I would still lose—hundreds of hours, and tens of thousands of dollars in legal bills. That's not an accident, that's one of the tools of these commissions. Every journalist in the country has been taught a lesson: Censor yourself now, or be put through a costly wringer. I said all this and then Officer McGovern replied, "You're entitled to your opinions, that's for sure."

But that's not for sure, is it? We're only entitled to our opinions now if they don't offend some very easily offended people.[1]

That is the very lesson author Mark Steyn had thrust upon him. Steyn is a well-known conservative columnist and author who is from Canada but now lives in the United States. His book *America Alone: The End of the World as We Know It* was a huge best seller that documented the many ways in which Western nations are slowly surrendering to Islam and Sharia.

Mr. Steyn and venerable old *Maclean's* magazine (founded in 1905) found themselves facing not one but two different Human Rights Commissions in Canada. The crime? Publishing an excerpt of Steyn's book in the magazine.

A group called the Canadian Islamic Congress (CIC) was deeply, profoundly wounded by Mr. Steyn's observations about some of the more radical adherents of Islam. The leaders of the CIC managed to rouse themselves from their swoon of offense long enough to demand that the magazine give them free space for a five-page rebuttal (which the magazine would not be allowed to edit) *and*—get this—the right to create the cover art for that issue of the magazine.

For some strange reason *Maclean's* chose not to turn control of their century-old publishing institution over to a bunch of thin-skinned know-nothings. So they and Steyn were forced into a forum to defend not their actions, but rather their motivation, intentions, feelings, and thoughts.

This is precisely the kind of grilling Ezra Levant faced. One of the first questions Levant was asked in his initial hearing was, "…what was your intent and purpose of your article?" As Levant later observed:

> It wasn't even a question about what we had published in the magazine. It was a question about my private thoughts. I asked her why my private feelings were of interest to the government. She said, very calmly, that they would be a factor taken into account by the government in determining whether or not I was guilty.[2]

Like Levant, Mark Steyn and the editors of *Maclean's* faced more than potential fines to the government and payments to offended parties; they could also have been forced to apologize for having unacceptable political or religious opinions.

What is the big deal about an apology? Well, think about it. As Ezra Levant has rightly pointed out, "Ordering a person—or a magazine—to say or publish words that they don't believe is an Orwellian act of thought control. The editor of *Maclean's*, Ken Whyte, maintains his magazine is fair. But human rights commissions have the power to order him to publish a confession that he's a bigot—or, as in one Ontario case, even order someone to study Islam. Even convicted murderers cannot be 'ordered' to apologize."[3]

One of Canada's many HRC policemen…er, sorry…policepersons is a man named Dean Steacy, the principal "anti-hate" investigator for the HRC. In one hearing he was asked what value he placed upon freedom of speech when investigating a case of hurt feelings. His reply?

"Freedom of speech is an American concept, so I don't give it any value. It's not my job to give value to an American concept."[4]

Here's the problem. Freedom of speech (or of the press or of association, for that matter) was not invented out of thin air by America's Founding Fathers. Such freedoms were part of a centuries-old English tradition derived from both Judeo-Christian ideals and the Enlightenment. This is a tradition that Canada, as a British commonwealth, clearly shares—or used to share.

What Mr. Steacy and the rest of his hate-hunting ilk apparently don't understand is that those icky "American" freedoms of which he is so dismissive are the legs on which his fragile democracy stands—and he is actively sawing them off.

As Mark Steyn commented:

> Mr. Steacy is wrong. It is not "freedom of speech" that is the kinky foreign imposition but his own Orwellian "human rights" regime, set up in the late 1970s and wholly alien to Canada's legal tradition. Why he is so unacquainted with English law as to believe "freedom of speech" is an "American concept" is something I look forward to exploring with him face to face.[5]

All of this, of course, is liberal political correctness, multiculturalism, and "tolerance" run stark-raving amok. Frighteningly, there are many here in the United States who would like nothing better than to establish an American version of these thought-policing, so-called human rights commissions. Many university campuses already have them and are helping to make our great centers of learning some of the *least* intellectually free places in our land.

But Canada is ahead of us on this one. To get a glimpse of where we might be headed, note that a pastor in Alberta wrote a letter to the editor expressing his opinion that homosexuality was a sin. Upon its publication, the letter offended a local teacher. So, did he submit a vigorous rebuttal for publication in the paper? No, he filed a complaint with the HRC, which ruled the pastor's letter "likely to expose gay persons to more hatred in the community."[6] The pastor was convicted; thankfully the ruling against him was later overturned. However, the law under which he was prosecuted remains "on the books."[7]

Is it possible that in Canada—one of the great democracies of the Western world—we are witnessing the slow death of free speech and freedom of the press? I'm afraid so.

We've been impacted personally by this frightening trend. When these developments began in Canada, we had to take a hard look at our television programming that went north of the border and make some difficult decisions about how we would continue to preach the gospel in such a chilling atmosphere.

You can be sure that rational journalists and politicians will think twice before criticizing the creeping imposition of Sharia law in Canada. And then they'll think of something else they can write about—something safe.

You see, unkind words might hurt someone's feelings. And Big Mother is listening.

PRETTY BABIES

B ACK IN 1978 a Brooke Shields movie raised a lot of eyebrows and quite a few hackles—and rightly so.

Shields, who was twelve at the time, portrayed a twelve-year-old girl growing up inside a New Orleans brothel in 1917. In the film Shields's character is shown posing for nude photographs. Eventually her virginity is auctioned off to the highest bidding "gentleman" customer.

The public outcry the movie triggered showed that, in the late 1970s, our culture still had a few moral mooring ropes lashed to the dock of sanity—even though progressive types had been hacking at them furiously since the launch of the sexual revolution a decade earlier.

Today, what some have called "the sexualization of childhood" is not only rampant; it is a multibillion-dollar pop culture industry. Here is how a *Washington Post* article under the headline "Goodbye to Girlhood" described it:

> Ten-year-old girls can slide their low-cut jeans over "eye-candy" panties. French maid costumes, garter belt included, are available in preteen sizes. Barbie now comes in a "bling-bling" style, replete with halter top and go-go boots. And it's not unusual for girls under 12 to sing, "Don't cha wish your girlfriend was hot like me?"
>
> American girls, say experts, are increasingly being fed a cultural catnip of products and images that promote looking and acting sexy.[1]

The article was prompted by a troubling report from the American Psychological Association's (APA) Task Force on the Sexualization of Girls, which pointed out that girls are relentlessly "depicted in a sexualizing manner" in pretty much every medium available, including TV shows, magazines, and music videos.[2]

First of all, how far down the road to perdition has a nation staggered when it has organizations like the APA having to commission a task force to point out the manifold ways the popular culture pressures and entices little girls to tart themselves up like dance hall floozies on Saturday night?

Do you think I'm exaggerating?

Ask any parent who has enrolled a little girl in dance class lately. Most I've spoken to said they were hard-pressed to find a dance studio that didn't want to turn their seven- or eight-year-old into a gyrating, bumping, grinding Laker Girl.

The toy marketers are valiantly doing their part in the war on innocence too. A horrified mom in Australia wrote about the Bratz line of dolls for girls (an American export) in a newspaper there:

> So THIS is the end product—little girls dressed as sex bait.... It's an intelligent parent's nightmare—and a pervert's dream. Bratz are childlike dolls—all big eyes and big heads—packaged as hookers. They have pouting lips, bare midriffs, plunging tops, tiny skirts and skimpy lingerie in black and pink.
>
> The dolls look like tarts and you can buy the clothes to make your little girl look just the same at any number of fashion outlets. Who would want to do that? Well, apparently lots of people would. Department stores aren't known for stocking stuff that no one will want to buy.... What are they thinking of, these mothers who turn their little girls into sex kittens?[3]

Dads in Houston aren't viewing the Bratz dolls any more favorably. One asked, "Why on earth would I want my daughters, still in single digits age-wise, to be playing with dolls that make immodesty all the rage? The first one that appeared in my house—courtesy of another friend of my daughter—wore a thong under the mini-est of mini skirts."[4]

Clothing? Sadly, we're in a culture where the typical male or female under the age of twenty-five can't name even one Supreme Court justice but can tell you the names of two or three Victoria's Secret catalog models. In such a society it shouldn't surprise us to see trouble trickling down to fashions aimed at little girls.

One place it seems to consistently trickle in is at your local mall's Abercrombie & Fitch clothing store. The trendy retailer has made a fortune selling clothing to high school and college-aged young people in stores filled with giant photographs of barely dressed young models shown, shall we say, getting to know each other.

The fact is, the clothing company has a history of pushing the boundaries of decency and good taste and then enjoying the publicity windfall that comes its way from the resulting controversy. Some suspect that shocking "uncool" moms and dads is at the heart of the chain's marketing and branding strategy.

That's why, when the company sought to extend its brand to a younger audience and opened a chain of stores (under the name *Abercrombie*) for kids aged seven through fourteen, few were surprised at the outcome: the store started crossing lines and violating taboos like a drunken frat boy on his first spring break.

To be specific, in 2002 Abercrombie stores rolled out a line of thong underwear for elementary school-aged girls that might be described as "pedophile-chic."[5] You see, the thongs came imprinted with artwork and slogans such as "eye candy" and "wink wink." A company spokeswoman defended the line, calling it "cute and fun and sweet."[6]

The overall cuteness and sweetness of having their baby girls marketed to in a way that encourages them to think of themselves as legitimate objects of sexual desire was lost on most parents. But then, we're *so* behind the times here in flyover country.

As one mom told a reporter for the *Milwaukee Journal Sentinal*: "It's out of hand at this point. It really is. It's Frederick's of Hollywood for preteens and teenagers." In a comment from another mom quoted in the same article, we find one of the roots of the problem. She said, "I think of myself as fairly hip, and I think it's just disgusting."[7]

In that remark you find one of the two great fears keeping most parents from taking a stand against this insanity. Parents are petrified of being viewed as un-hip. That's right. You can call anyone almost anything these days and get away with it. But if you want to start a fist fight, accuse the typical American parent of being a fuddy-duddy.

And in this postmodern era, parents are equally terrified of being seen as judgmental.

So, a generation of parents allows their twin paralyzing phobias—the fears of being labeled either un-cool or intolerant—to bind and gag them as they watch their daughters follow a suicidal, oversexed culture over a cliff. It makes perfect sense.

Of course, when a guy like me points out trends like this, it triggers a lot of eye-rolling and chortling about how previous generations thought Elvis's hips were a menace to public morals and how Barbara Eden wasn't allowed to show her belly button on *I Dream of Jeanie*.

Let them chortle. Back in those days (which weren't so very long ago) we didn't have pedophiles trolling the Internet trying to find their next victim on a social networking Web site or sex slavers patrolling the malls of suburbia looking for young girls to kidnap and sell into a life of sexual bondage, drug addiction, and premature death.

Someone has to point out that girls (and boys for that matter) naturally have a powerful desire to fit in. Unfortunately, "fitting in" these days means abandoning innocence and adopting a strip-club sensibility.

Do you think I'm exaggerating again? Judge for yourself.

A few years ago the British retailer Tesco (which recently opened its first U.S. stores) was forced to remove a pole-dancing kit from the toys and games section of its online store. The sales pitch for the product on the Tesco Web site said, "Unleash the sex kitten inside...simply extend the Peekaboo pole inside the tube, slip on the sexy tunes and away you go! Soon you'll be flaunting it to the world and earning a fortune in Peekaboo Dance Dollars."[8]

Charming.

The kit came complete with extendible chrome pole, a "sexy dance garter," and an instructional DVD of "suggestive dance moves."[9] By the way, actually the pole and music are really enough to elicit the desired response from a preteen. Let these two incentives go and a fallen and depraved nation will do the rest.

Where are the feminists when you need them? It seems that while the sisterhood was either obsessively fighting to keep America safe for late-term abortionists or demanding that every university offer a gay-lesbian-bisexual-transgender degree track in women's studies programs, an entire generation of girls happily bought into the lie that the highest ideal to which a girl can aspire is "hotness."

It's enough to make a Susan B. Anthony dollar weep real tears.

LIBRARIANS FOR DEFILEMENT

C ONSIDER THE FOLLOWING premise: "There is nothing in print or on the Internet anywhere in the world that a child should not have unfettered access to—and without having to have a parent's permission."

Does that sound a tad extreme to you?

Well, keep that radical view in mind the next time you see a sweet, spectacled librarian sitting behind a desk. It may or may not be her (or his) personal position, but it captures the essence of the organization that strongly influences the policies, procedures, and values of that branch.

I'm referring to the powerful American Library Association (ALA). For decades the ALA has worked in close partnership with the American Civil Liberties Union (ACLU) to label as outrageous censorship any local communities' attempts to influence the choice of books on their library shelves and the kinds of materials to which children should have easy access.

You see, parents have the annoying tendency to insist on having a say over what their kids see and read. And the very taxpayers whose hard-earned dollars underwrite the libraries obnoxiously think that they should be able to influence the product they're paying for.

That is why anyone who dares challenge the ALA's sacrosanct "any book, any time, at any age" orthodoxy will be in for a lot of shaming and over-the-top hysterics about Nazi book burnings and George Orwell and *Fahrenheit 451*.

Yes, allow a parent to question the appropriateness of shelving a profanity-laced sex-fest amid the Fiction for Young Teens section, and Brownshirts will soon be goose-stepping through the stacks on their way to toasting marshmallows in a bonfire of Nancy Drew mysteries.

If city council members are allowed to question the wisdom of spending scarce budget resources on *Candace Has Three Dads, Two Moms and a "Special Friend"* instead of replacing the tattered copy of *The Secret Garden*, then we're surely only weeks away from seeing theocrats clear the shelves of every book but the King James Bible, Jerry Falwell's autobiography, and a few Chick tracts.

For decades the ALA, which wields enormous influence over the administrators and staff of the nation's libraries, has consistently positioned itself as the courageous and principled levee holding back the ignorant tide of narrow-minded censors who want to ban *Huckleberry Finn* and *Catcher in the Rye*.

The centerpiece of this posturing is the ALA's annual Banned Books Week. It's a yearly opportunity for the group to preen about intellectual freedom and send out press releases listing the "Top Ten Most Frequently Challenged Books" of the year (with a "100 Most Frequently Challenged Books of the Decade" list appearing every tenth year).[1] They organize "Read Outs!" in which people sit around and read naughty novels and encourage us all to "get hooked on a banned book."[2]

Here's the odd thing, though. None of the "banned books" have actually been, you know…*banned*. What the ALA obsessively records and uses to generate its much-publicized lists are challenges to books. A challenge to a book occurs when someone walks up to a librarian with a copy of *How to Have Wild Teen Sex and Hide It From Your Parents* and asks, "Why is my neighborhood library carrying this trash?" Score! Another book has been challenged. The book's title is recorded and dutifully reported to HQ.

In any discussion of censorship, the organization will invariably mention how the knuckle-dragging fundamentalist book-banners have even opposed *The Adventures of Huckleberry Finn* in the past.[3] What they don't mention is that past challenges to *Huck Finn* have come from African Americans concerned about the book's use of the "*N* word" and its portrayal of black folks in what is now seen as a stereotypical fashion.

The ALA's own statistics show that the vast majority of all challenges come from parents.[4] A significant percentage of these involve complaints that certain books are, to use the organization's term, "unsuited to any age group." In other words, in spite of the way the ALA likes to characterize their virtuous battle, it's generally not the case that intolerant mobs want to keep other adults from reading whatever they jolly well please. It's that parents frequently object to having books containing sex, homosexuality, Satanism, or sadistic violence accessible to kids too young to handle them.

Here is the real irony in all this. Over the years, the ALA has fought a losing battle in state legislatures to keep parents from being able to access the circulation records of their children. The ALA's longstanding position is that children have privacy rights and parents should only have access to their child's circulation records when fines are owed. In other words, "We're happy to let you pay the bills, but otherwise butt out."

For example, when it looked like the Alaska State Senate was about to pass a bill that would require public libraries to give parents access to their children's records upon request, the state branch of the ALA worked hard to weaken the statute as much as possible. As the ALA's own newsletter reported:

> Lynn Shepherd, chair of the Alaska Library Association's Government Relations Committee, said the group would like to see amendments to the measure that would allow library records to be released to parents if a child's books are overdue but require children's written permission for parents to see other records or pick up books for them. "We recognize there needs to be a balance of parents' rights, children's rights, library staff rights, and the protection of public property," Shepherd said....[5]

That's so upside down, I'm dizzy from simply quoting it!

Enter the bizarre world of the ALA where the idea that parents have a right to know what books their children have checked out is scandalous. It's an upside-down realm where parent's rights have to be carefully balanced with "children's rights."

An ALA "Q & A" document on "Intellectual Freedom and Censorship" states: "The primary responsibility for rearing children rests with parents.

If parents want to keep certain ideas or forms of expression away from their children, they must assume the responsibility for shielding those children."[6]

So, which is it? When confronted with the prospect of children accessing inappropriate material, the ALA glibly says, "Hey, it's the parent's responsibility." But when parents try to exercise that responsibility, the ALA says, "It's none of your business. Children have privacy rights."

Understood?

Such contortions of logic and principle were forced to new extremes when libraries started offering free Internet access to their patrons.

Given the ALA's deeply ingrained anti-censorship reflexes, it is not surprising to learn that libraries deeply resented any suggestions from the taxpaying public that they put pornography-filtering software on their computers.

For example, in 2001, in response to national legislation mandating some modest level of porn filtering in libraries receiving federal funds, the ALA, with their bosom buddies the ACLU and other fellow travelers such as People for the American Way, issued a joint statement in opposition.

How extreme is this knee-jerk opposition to common sense safeguards? Judith Krug, director of the ALA's Office of Intellectual Freedom said: "Blocking material leads to censorship. That goes for pornography and bestiality, too. If you don't like it, don't look at it.... Every time I hear someone say, I want to protect the children, I want to pull my hair out."[7]

Well...I want to protect the children, I want to protect the children...there, I just saved you a cut and style!

Early in the fight, the ALA labeled such online safeguards "Censorware." Amusingly, civil liberties groups have tended to think that if they can just attach some form of the word *censorship* to an issue, it will shut down debate. Nevertheless, the organization has been losing this battle as well. As the accuracy and sophistication of filtering software has increased, state after state has enacted its own filtering mandates.

Still, the ALA continues to fight even the most modest attempts by parents and communities to guide book selection and availability—all in the name of intellectual freedom. Which would make it pretty hypocritical if the ALA were committing its own brand of censorship of unpopular ideas, wouldn't it?

Sure it would. Yet the news site World Net Daily reported that the ALA's governing council was considering severing all ties with the Boy Scouts of America because they found the Scouts' policies regarding homosexuals and atheists offensive.[8]

When a group of Cuban librarians who had been jailed by the Castro dictatorship for circulating unauthorized books such as George Orwell's *Animal Farm* turned to the ALA for advocacy help, the group turned them down cold.[9] It seems left-wing solidarity with Castro trumps intellectual freedom when it comes right down to it.

With even more blatant two-facedness, the ALA aided and abetted a high-tech lynching of Ohio State University librarian Scott Savage, who'd had the gall to suggest a conservative book, *The Marketing of Evil*, be added to the campus-wide reading list. Scott actually ended up being accused of sexual harassment because the book he'd recommended contained some statements critical of the homosexual rights agenda.[10]

So much for the courageous defense of ideas and speech no matter how unpopular. I guess it's only censorship when Christians or conservatives are the ones who find something offensive.

Do I wish some Christian parents would think before they try to organize a movement to have *Harry Potter* or *Heather Has Two Mommies* pulled from library shelves? Yes, I do. It only validates stereotypes of Christians as intolerant scolds trying to impose their values on everyone else.

But the ALA can't have it both ways. It should either empower parents to make decisions for their children and be accountable for what their children are seeing, or build in some system-wide protections to keep young eyes from seeing things they're not yet ready to see.

The American Library Association will tolerate neither. Ask why, and you just might find yourself labeled a "book banner."

By the way, the last time I checked, the most banned book on the planet was the Bible. But I don't think that's what they have in mind when they talk about reading banned books.

MAKE ROOM FOR NANNY

A PEOPLE CAN BE free, or they can be taken care of—but they can't be both.

This, in so many words, was the powerful "limited government," anti-socialist message of Ronald Reagan. The fortieth president knew that asking for cradle-to-grave care from the state not only came at the price of personal liberty, but it was also a promise on which government simply could not deliver. Government bureaucracies are invariably less efficient, less effective, and less responsive than their private-sector counterparts, frequently making worse the ills they intend to cure.

Thus we got the Gipper's famous quip about what he called the nine most terrifying words in the English language: "I'm from the government, and I'm here to help."

Back in the 1980s it was tempting to believe that the Reagan Revolution had finally halted creeping socialism's advance (which during the FDR and LBJ years had actually done more galloping than creeping). That didn't turn out to be the case. After Reagan left office, the growth of government accelerated again, but it did so in what George H. W. Bush liked to call a "kinder, gentler" form.

This meant that government began to gather more power, control, and resources to itself for the motherly purpose of keeping us all safe and warm and healthy and happy.

Back in the 1940s, George Orwell described the future authoritarian government that would control all of our lives as "a boot stamping on a human face—forever."[1] The future we actually got was more like Mary Poppins jamming spoonfuls of sugar and medicine into a face forever.

Today many people unquestioningly view it as the proper role of government to address every aspect of every citizen's human needs. And many don't even limit the scope of that care to humans. What has come to be known as "the nanny state" increasingly extends to pets and wildlife too.

For these people, it is an article of faith that wherever life presents dangers, it is government's job to mitigate it. Where there are risks, regulations must be in place to minimize them. Where people's bad choices can result in negative consequences, it is the government's responsibility to coerce better decisions or, even better, make the choices for them. As we saw in chapter 21 ("Big Mother Is Listening"), when some people say things others don't want to hear, then government must force them to be quiet.

It used to be that it was exclusively liberals and so-called progressives who believed that the lips of government must kiss every boo-boo and make it all better. But in recent years this mind-set has become so universal that you're likely to hear it from both ends of the political spectrum and all points in between. Even President George Bush told a group of union workers in my home state of Ohio, "We have a responsibility that when somebody hurts, Government has got to move."[2]

Really? There was a time in this nation when, if somebody hurt, their family and friends had the "responsibility" to "move." And if there was no family nearby, neighbors moved or local church folks moved.

Faceless bureaucrats administering programs that are inefficient at best, and counterproductive at worst, weren't the presumed easers of a citizen's pain.

Today, at every level of government—from the halls of Congress to the city council chambers—thousands of laws and regulations designed to protect you from yourself are being crafted. And for every little piece of well-intentioned caretaking you are given, you surrender a commensurate quantity of precious, blood-bought liberty.

I tell people that I learned an important concept that has helped protect me from the day I discovered it until now—I learned to read. It's amazing what you can do for yourself if you take a little initiative. Of course, because of our national obsession with depending on someone else to protect us, some of the things we all have to read are a thousand disclaimers in legalese about the dangers of whatever product we have had the audacity to purchase—including the cup of coffee we get at the fast-food drive-through.

On the health front, New York City has banned the use of trans fats in restaurants. Chicago has outlawed foie gras. There are serious discussions currently underway about fining or penalizing people for being overweight. Also in New York, a recent law requires restaurants to make calorie counts of items as conspicuous as their prices—a requirement that author Jacob Sullum argues, "...forces restaurants to engage in a form of government-mandated nagging, intended to have the same effect as paying someone to whisper 'Are you *sure* you want fries with that?' in the ear of every customer contemplating his order."[3]

In California, a regulatory trendsetter that other states tend to follow, the protecting arms of state government are wrapping citizens in an ever-tightening embrace of care and concern. Like any good nanny would do for any helpless, clueless child in her care, California intends to make sure you eat right, don't play in the street, pick up after yourself, and take proper care of your hamster.

For example, San Francisco has an ordinance requiring dog "guardians" (it's now a no-no to refer to humans as owners of pets) to have clean water served in a non-spill bowl, located in the shade. That's right, Nancy Pelosi's home town now has a city ordinance telling dog owners what kind of bowl to use and where to place it. Somebody better tell the San Fran nannies about the sun's daily habit of moving across the sky and causing the precise location of the shade to move with it throughout the day. Better yet, don't say a word.

And don't walk that dog while listening to your iPod. Legislators in some cities are considering a ban on earbud headphones for everyone in order to keep a foolish few from stepping into traffic.

California is also leading the way in requiring new homes to have programmable thermostats that can be remotely controlled by the power company. In times of high demand, the utility provider will be able to reset your heating or cooling to the level it *ought* to be at rather than where you actually want it.

But it's not just California. Variations of all of these regulations and thousands of others are currently being considered in states and cities across America. And they all have one thing in common—they're for your own good, sweetie.

Any day now I fully expect to see a national taxpayer-funded initiative to "raise awareness" of the dangers of running with scissors, followed by government mandates setting speed guidelines for foot-based locomotion while transporting cutting implements.

Of course, it's a good idea to eat right, avoid trans fats, wear a helmet when you ride a bicycle, avoid stepping into highway traffic with "Death Cab for Cutie" blasting in your ears, and have clean, cool water for your schnauzer. But you can't *force* individuals to act prudently or wisely—or at least you can't do so and remain a free people.

G. K. Chesterton wrote: "The free man owns himself. He can damage himself with either eating or drinking; he can ruin himself with gambling. If he does he is certainly a [expletive] fool, and he might possibly be a [expletive] soul; but if he may not, he is not a free man any more than a dog."[4]

And as author Nick Gillespie has observed:

> ...these bans reduce all of us to the status of children, incapable of making informed choices. Is it quaint to suggest that there's something wrong with that in a country founded on the idea of the individual's rights to life, liberty, and the pursuit of happiness?[5]

Enlightened proponents of the nanny state want to see us become much more like the socialistic nations of Europe. Central governments there confiscate huge percentages of productive people's income in order to provide "free" health care for everyone along with never-ending unemployment benefits. This, while requiring employers to provide months of paid vacation, maternity leave, paternity leave, and a host of other mandated benefits to people they're not allowed to lay off under any circumstances and who want to retire at age fifty-five.

What people now want is an all-powerful saving benefactor who will guarantee them health, safety, income, long life, and protection from all calamity and misfortune. There is an old word for such an entity: the word is *messiah*.

Whether they realize it or not, that is precisely how a large number of people view their government in our day—as a messiah that will save them from everything. It's the new idolatry. If you doubt it, take a hard look at the outrage and bitterness that erupted against the federal government following Hurricane Katrina. Behind all the bluster about FEMA's response time and what the Army Corps of Engineers should or shouldn't have done with the levees around New Orleans, a clear assumption fueled the anger. That assumption is this: when one of the strongest hurricanes in decades hit one of the most vulnerable population centers in our nation, the death, destruction, and ensuing human suffering were the federal government's fault.

It used to be that natural disasters were called *acts of God*. In a way, I guess, they still are. It's just that people have found a new god. If so, they'd better get used to disappointment. The god they have chosen in their quest for healing, provision, and protection simply can't deliver the goods.

Yet there's good news. Standing by patiently is a real God who can deliver *and will*.

IT TAKES ~~A VILLAGE~~
TWO PARENTS

W HEN A POLITICIAN or policy advocate starts talking about doing something for the sake of *"our* children," it's a wise reflex to put your hand over your wallet and pray. You're about to get a little poorer and a little less free to raise your kids as you see fit.

The *"our* children" appeal was at the heart of Hillary Clinton's book *It Takes a Village*; it remains one of the most effective ways to stifle debate and foist more top-down, centralized control upon America's families.

Of course, if you're a parent, you may be excused for wondering just when *your* kids became the rightful property of the society at large. Did you sleep through the hearing where joint custody was awarded to a committee comprised of Oprah, the Children's Defense Fund (CDF), the Department of Education, and the U.S. Department of Health and Human Services?

After all, it was Hillary who, in an address to a church group, scolded: "As adults we have to start thinking and believing that *there isn't really any such thing as someone else's child....* For that reason, we cannot permit discussions of children and families to be subverted by political or ideological debate" (emphasis added).[1]

On *Face the Nation*, freshly installed House Speaker Nancy Pelosi told Bob Schieffer that when she took the Speaker's gavel, she took it "from the hands of the special interests and [put it] into the hands of America's children."[2]

You'll recall that it was zealous, utopian Marxists who destroyed

Russia's ability to feed itself by "collectivizing" farming. Today, a new wave of utopians wants to bring that same level of efficiency and excellence to parenting by collectivizing child rearing. I'm only exaggerating slightly. The fact is that those with the greatest faith in government's power to fix every problem have learned this: the best way to get people to surrender their prerogatives is to invoke the well-being of "The Children."

As syndicated columnist Jonah Goldberg has noted, this tactic "transforms children into a principle for which any violation of limited government is justified."[3] Goldberg also points out that it was the above-mentioned Children's Defense Fund, headed by Hillary's friend Marian Wright Edelman, which pioneered this style of demagoguery. Goldberg reminds us:

> The CDF was launched in the early 1970s largely to push for more generous social welfare programs. But Edelman realized that welfare could be a hard sell. "When you talked about poor people or black people, you faced a shrinking audience," she said. "I got the idea that children might be a very effective way to broaden the base for change." The idea was as simple as it was brilliant: By making The Children the beneficiaries of welfare rather than the adults, the Left could portray any attempt to curb the welfare state as "anti-child."[4]

That is precisely the playbook Team Welfare State has been following ever since.

Take, for instance, the landmark welfare reform legislation that President Clinton signed (to his everlasting credit) back in the 1990s. The Children's Defense Fund called the proposal an act of "national child abandonment" and "the domestic equivalent of bombing Vietnamese villages in order to save them."[5] But that response looks like a model of fair-minded restraint in comparison to the teeth-gnashing and wailing that rang through the halls of Congress. As one article on the tenth anniversary of the signing of the legislation recalled:

> Cries from Democrats of "anti-family," "anti-child," "mean-spir-ited," echoed through the Capitol, as did warnings of impending

Third World–style poverty: "children begging for money, children begging for food, eight- and nine-year-old prostitutes," as New Jersey senator Frank Lautenberg put it. "They are coming for the children," Congressman John Lewis of Georgia wailed—"coming for the poor, coming for the sick, the elderly and disabled." Congressman William Clay of Missouri demanded, "What's next? Castration?" Senator Ted Kennedy called it "legislative child abuse," Senator Chris Dodd, "unconscionable," Senator Daniel Patrick Moynihan—in what may well be the lowest point of an otherwise miraculous career—"something approaching an Apocalypse."[6]

Gee, it's a good thing they didn't embarrass themselves by overreacting or anything.

More than a decade later, it turns out that the legislation had pretty much all the positive effects its backers said it would, and then some—with not a hint of the cataclysmic ones the detractors so confidently predicted. It has lowered the number of women and children living in dependence upon the government, slashed the number of children living below the poverty line, and, most significantly, lowered the rates of illegitimacy that were devastating inner-city family structure and fueling an epidemic of fatherlessness.

Nevertheless, the Edelman strategy remains the preferred approach. For example, the more recent debate over expanding federal funding of S-CHIP (a program that sends federal money to states for providing health insurance to families with children) has prompted welfare-staters to bring the billy club of The Children back out to pummel the head and shoulders of anyone who opposes additional federal spending.

For example, California Congressman Pete Stark got so worked up about it that he went for a liberal moonbat trifecta—slamming conservative heartlessness toward children, the war in Iraq's futility, *and* President Bush's bloodthirstiness, all in one rhetorical flourish:

> The Republicans are worried that they can't pay for insuring an additional 10 million children. They sure don't care about finding $200 billion to fight the illegal war in Iraq.... Where are you going

to get that money? ... You don't have money to fund the war on children, but you're going to spend it to blow up innocent people if we can get enough kids to grow old enough for you to send to Iraq to get their heads blown off for the president's amusement.[7]

Got that? If you oppose extending what is supposed to be a lifeline for poor families to those who aren't actually poor, you're just a couple of clicks shy of being the kind of monster who finds amusement in kids getting their heads blown off. You know—like the former president of the United States. Position noted. I suppose Emperor Caligula and Vlad the Impaler were opposed to middle-class entitlement creep too.

For the record, after being robustly condemned across the political spectrum, Stark eventually apologized for the "president's amusement" part of his remarks. But keep in mind the wise Bible saying, "Out of the abundance of the heart [the] mouth speaks."[8] That was Jesus's way of reminding us that what we *really* think tends to leak out at inopportune times.

Still, in spite of the best efforts of the self-styled advocates for *our children*, most parents stubbornly continue to think of their children as *their* responsibility. And as both common sense and research suggest, the more parents feel responsible for their children, the better off children are. That means any attempts by government to relieve parents of some of their responsibilities—no matter how well intentioned—will end up hurting kids in the long run.

Another thing the research makes clear is that when it comes to the well-being of children, two parents are better than one.

Nevertheless, in true upside-down fashion, the Left continues to champion policies, programs, and social trends that undermine traditional marriage, destigmatize divorce, encourage transitory cohabitation, and normalize single parenthood—all to the detriment of children.

In 2005, the left-leaning Brookings Institution published a report that confirmed what embattled pro-family, traditional-values advocates had been saying for decades. Namely, that children do better with a mom *and* a dad.

The Future of Children, a journal published by Brookings and Princeton

University's Woodrow Wilson School, summarized: "Staying together for the sake of the children might not be such a bad idea after all....Children from two-parent families are better off emotionally, socially, and economically."[9]

Numerous other reports clearly show how devastating divorce is on many kids. For example, the Heritage Foundation has reported that children raised in intact families have, on average, higher academic achievement, better emotional health, and fewer behavioral problems.[10]

I'm not suggesting that if you are a single parent or have a divorce in your background, your kids are doomed. But what is abundantly clear is that any person or group claiming to care about the welfare of children should be rooting for a revival of the traditional two-parent family. But don't hold your breath.

As Mark Steyn has asked:

> So what is the best thing America could do "for the children"? Well, it could try not to make the same mistake as most of the rest of the Western world and avoid bequeathing the next generation a system of unsustainable entitlements that turns the entire nation into a giant Ponzi scheme.[11]

Indeed. Unfortunately, that logic wasn't apparent in Hillary Clinton's campaign-trail suggestion of giving "every baby born in America a $5,000 account that will grow over time."[12] Do the math on that. Given the roughly four million births here each year, Clinton's proposal would have cost taxpayers some $20 billion annually.

Sure. Let the Ponzi scheme continue. It's for the sake of *our* children."

ACADEMIC ADOLESCENCE

D EAD WHITE MEN."
These three words have come to serve as efficient shorthand for the academic Left's disdainful dismissal of our entire heritage as a civilization. In a protest at Stanford back in the 1980s, multicultural and feminist protesters famously chanted, "Hey hey, ho ho, Western culture's got to go."

To a large degree Western culture has gone quietly, at least where our once-great universities are concerned. Those departed male Caucasians—Aristotle, Plato, the apostle Paul, Augustine, da Vinci, Locke, Hume, Madison, Dostoevsky—have moved aside for gender studies, sexuality studies, peace studies, transnational feminist perspectives, and classes such as Cornell University's "Bodies Politic: Queer Theory and Literature of the Body."

What you increasingly *won't* find on many campuses is the freedom to express or explore conservative ideas. Of all the institutions in America, the university should be a place where the free exchange of ideas is most welcomed, even celebrated. Yet somehow, some way, America's university campuses have largely become the least intellectually free zones in our nation. You'll find more academic curiosity and enlightenment at a WWE pro wrestling spectacular than at the typical elite liberal arts college these days. By the way, my money is on Rey Mysterio.

For example, in October of 2007, conservative author David Horowitz was invited by the College Republicans of Emory University in Atlanta to deliver a speech on radical Islam as a part of Islamofascism Awareness Week. From the outset Horowitz was interrupted by shouts and chants from campus protestors who had packed the auditorium. About twenty minutes into the event, the crowd got so out of hand that police had to be called in and Horowitz escorted off stage.

Among the protestors were the usual Left suspects, including campus members of Amnesty International, Veterans for Peace, and Students for Justice in Palestine. Actively involved in the shout-down were members of a group called—get this now—the National Project to Defend Dissent & Critical Thinking in Academia.[1] (Let's pause a moment to let that sink in.)

There, in one little incident, you discover everything you need to know about the Far Left's approach to free speech issues on campus. Most left-wingers appear utterly deaf to the screaming irony of calling yourself a defender of dissent and critical thinking and marching off to shout down the academic speech of an established intellectual—simply because you don't think you're going to like what he has to say.

Afterward the university president issued an apology to Horowitz and the College Republicans and promised to take steps to ensure that the next speaker got a respectful hearing. Here's the problem with that. The next scheduled speaker was a left-wing apologist for Palestinian terrorist groups. That prompted Robert Spencer, a respected scholar of Islamic history, theology, and law to rhetorically ask the president of Emory a few questions:

> [D]oes your determination to make sure Hanan Ashrawi's speech goes off without disruption have anything to do with her status as an apologist for Palestinian jihad terror against Israel?
>
> And aren't your precautions regarding her speech a suggestion that conservative students are likely to engage in the same fascist silencing tactics that the Emory student Leftists engaged in when they torpedoed Horowitz's speech?
>
> Yet where and when have conservative students *ever* behaved in such a manner?[2]

Great "heads up" questions. Especially that last one. One of the premier conceits and self-deceptions of the Left is that conservatives pose a grave threat to free speech and that Leftists represent a courageous bulwark of defense against them. It's a theme self-righteous Hollywood loves to work into films at every opportunity.

Yet, as Robert Spencer suggests, one is hard-pressed to find a single case of a Leftist speech being disrupted by rowdy campus conservatives. Whereas conservatives are constantly and repeatedly shouted down (on the rare occasions they are invited to speak at all) by loudmouth "activists."

The list of conservatives who have faced this kind of bullying and harassment is long indeed and includes Horowitz, Ann Coulter, Condoleeza Rice, Jeane Kirkpatrick, Dick Cheney, Clarence Thomas, Antonin Scalia, and Daniel Pipes, just to name a few.

Rich Lowry of *National Review* provided us all with a rare glimpse of this ugly brand of boorish harassment as he "live-blogged" the graduation ceremony from the liberal New School University in New York City. Laptop open, he recorded what he heard as Senator John McCain delivered a commencement address that Mark Salter described as "a beautiful prose poem to America, national service, and civil debate."

Here is an excerpt of Salter's notes:

> [McCain says,] "I supported the war in Iraq." Boos. Explains the war was not for cheap oil. A little heckling: "You're full of it!" Says he thought the "country's interest and values demanded" the war. Someone shouts: "Wrongly!" Someone else: "More poetry!" (A reference to lines from Yeats McCain had quoted earlier.)
>
> He says "whether [the war] was necessary or not...we all should shed a tear" for those who have sacrificed in it. Some hissing. Shouting.
>
> He eventually enters into a Bushian rift: "All people share the desire to be free"; "human rights are above the state and beyond history"; we are "insisting that all people have the right to be free." Someone shouts: "We're graduating, not voting!" Lots of derisive shouts and laughter and applause.
>
> As McCain continues with a personal story, a student shouts: "It's about my life, not yours."
>
> McCain: "When I was a young man, I thought glory was the highest value..." Groans from the students. "It's not about you!" "Sit down!"

McCain circles back around to the theme of civility: "We are not enemies, we are compatriots…" Boos, shouts. McCain: It "should remain an argument among friends"; we should be "respectful of the goodness in each other." Literally one person applauds.

McCain goes on to tell his story about his reconciliation with an opponent of the Vietnam War: "I had a friend once…" Groans, boos.

He talks about forgiving his friend who dissented from the war. Hostile rumblings from the students.

He says after the reconciliation, he and his friend "worked together for shared ideals." A shout: "We don't share your ideals!" As McCain closes there is a mix of boos and applause, and a few people even stand to clap.[3]

Keep Senator McCain's experience in mind the next time you hear some Leftist prattle on about how a progressive education instills in students a principled commitment to freedom of expression and a respect for ideas.

On the rare occasions that a liberal Democrat is heckled, it is often by those even farther to the Left—as when Madeleine Albright was interrupted by antiwar protesters at a Smith College commencement address. And I'm sure you recall the incident that launched a million YouTube viewings in which Senator John Kerry was interrupted by Andrew "Don't Tase Me Bro" Meyer during a Q & A at the University of Florida. Mr. Meyer's beef with Kerry, expressed loudly before he was robustly "tased" into silence (despite his impassioned pleas to his campus security "bro"), seemed to involve three points: a dispute over the outcome of the 2004 presidential election, Kerry's refusal to get on board the "impeach Bush" bandwagon, and Kerry's membership in Yale's secretive Skull and Bones organization.[4] The issues were near-fetishes with the left-wing denizens of the comment threads on HuffingtonPost.com, DailyKos.com, and DemocraticUnderground.com.

It's funny though—when conservative speakers are being screamed at, campus security seems remarkably reticent to whip out the tasers.

In fact, when liberals tried to shut down a speech by Ann Coulter at Syracuse University, the host College Republicans started to remove hecklers from the hall. As Coulter recalls, school administrators "blocked them from removing students disrupting the speech on the grounds that removing students screaming during a speech would violate the hecklers' 'free speech.' They had a 'free speech' right to prevent anyone from hearing a conservative's 'free speech.'"[5]

At the same time, students or teachers who dare to express crazy views like, oh, that America is *not* the locus of all evil in the world, or Islamic extremism may indeed pose more of a threat to our freedoms than do pro-life grandmothers, frequently find themselves in hot water.

Take the case of the Brandeis professor who was accused of using "insensitive terminology" in class. On today's university campus, nothing calls down the wrath of the P.C. police like the crime of insensitivity. It is instructive that the reflex of the Brandeis administration wasn't to stand up for intellectual freedom. It was to essentially order the professor off to a reeducation camp. (They called it "anti-discrimination training.") Regarding the Brandeis case, National Review Online's academia-oriented Phi Beta Cons blog noted:

> As we have seen with many other events in academe lately, administrators often have no sense of proportionality. If members of any preferred minority group issue some complaint, they go bananas trying to appease them. Evidently the "commitment to diversity" that's now obligatory in higher ed means that you can never say "no" to those groups, no matter how slight the provocation.[6]

Throughout the country, universities have attempted to discipline, censure, or outright shut down conservative campus newspapers that provide an alternative to the reliably left-wing "official" paper overseen by the reliably left-wing journalism faculty.

Invariably, professors and students only get the full backing (or at least backside covering) of the administration when they come down on conservative or Christian thought and speech.

In his excellent book *Persecution: How Liberals Are Waging War Against Christianity*, David Limbaugh relates the story of Texas Tech biology professor Michael Dini, who, for a time, refused to write medical school letters of recommendation for even the most outstanding of students unless they affirmed a belief in the theory of evolution. As Limbaugh relates:

> Dr. James Brink, the university's assistant provost, supported Dini. "I think a student with a strong faith and belief in creationism should not attend a public university," said Brink, "but rather should attend a Biblically grounded university where their ideas are reinforced instead of scientifically challenged."[7]

In other words, Christian parents in Texas should have their tax dollars appropriated to underwrite the operation of public universities in Texas, but their children should not avail themselves of those schools unless they are prepared to abandon their faith. Got it? Got it!

Fortunately, the Liberty Legal Institute took action against Texas Tech and Dini for what the suit described as "open religious bigotry." Dini rethought his policy and now only requires "that students be able to explain the theory of evolution, without requiring them to affirm their personal belief in its validity."[8]

Finally, there is the well-documented and widely recognized tendency in academia to indoctrinate malleable young minds with the most ludicrous and extreme liberal ideologies.

Did you know, for example, that Beethoven's revered Ninth Symphony is an expression of repressive patriarchal culture and carries an underlying theme of rape? Neither did I, until a *U.S. News and World Report* article pointed me to the writings of UCLA musicology professor Susan McClary.[9]

You can be sure her students get a heaping helping of the themes she outlines in her book *Feminine Endings*, including: "musical constructions of gender and sexuality,"[10] "gendered aspects of traditional music theory,"[11] "music as a gendered discourse,"[12] and "discursive strategies of women musicians."[13]

Now, I have listened to Beethoven's Ninth many times, and, for the life of me, I've never picked up on the patriarchal overtones or themes of dominance. But then I've not had the benefit of sitting through a UCLA music course that is as much about feminist indoctrination as it is about actual music.

Nor have I had to attend University of Northern Colorado professor Robert Dunkley's criminology course in which he gives essay exams requiring students to "make the argument that the military action of the U.S. attacking Iraq was criminal," "make the case for gay marriage," and "explain how this additional type of family could help prevent crime."[14] I suspect I would not do well in Professor Dunkley's class given my well-known proclivity to say precisely what I think.

The same would probably be true if I took Professor Priya Parmar's education class at Brooklyn College. There she advises instructors to "use rap [music] to teach English to children as young as eight, that standard English is a form of white oppression of blacks, and that those who disagree with her views should not become teachers."[15] I, on the other hand, would argue that those who *do* agree with her view should not become teachers. But that's just me.

Let's all say a prayer for the students who move through University of Michigan professor of anthropology Gayle Rubin's classroom. In addition to being a widely read feminist author, she is the founder of Samois, the first publicly recognized lesbian sadomasochism club. Using the book *The Lesbian and Gay Studies Reader*, she asserts that "the government's pursuit of child molesters is 'a savage and undeserved witch hunt.'"[16]

While you're on your knees, you might also want to mention the students exposed to the deep thoughts of Grover Furr, a humanities professor at Montclair State University in New Jersey. He requires his students to use his Web site as a reference resource. There they find gems like: "What the majority of humanity needs today is an International like the Communist International to coordinate the fight against exploitation—just as the IMF and World Bank, Exxon and Reebok, the U.S. and French coordinate the fight FOR exploitation."[17]

As Michael Barone soberly reminds us:

> On campuses, students are bombarded with denunciations of dead white males and urged to engage in the deconstruction of all past

learning and scholarship. Not all of this takes, of course. Most students have enough good sense to see that the campus radicals' description of the world is wildly at odds with reality. But this battering away at ideas of truth and goodness does have some effect. Very many of our university graduates emerge with the default assumption thoroughly wired into their mental software. And, it seems, they carry it with them for most of their adult lives.[18]

Citing egregious examples of left-wing indoctrination is really too easy. It's like shooting fish in a barrel. (Which I would never do, of course, because guns are bad and fish have rights and feelings.) Nevertheless, these and the thousands of other examples I could cite manage to be simultaneously silly and sinister.

But at the core, there is a fundamental *childishness* about all this.

The outrageous course offerings selected mainly for their shock value, the labeling of conservative criticism of diversity-run-amok as "hate speech," the constant dubious claims to being victims of censorship while actively censoring others, the pretentious pose of fighting "the establishment" when they *are* the establishment, the reflexive hatred of all things American and Western...it's all so very...well, juvenile.

Like grown-ups, conservatives generally want nothing more than an opportunity to debate ideological opponents, either on paper or in organized forums following established orderly formats.

Increasingly, campus liberals just want their opponents to shut the [expletive] up.

27

WHEN MANLINESS IS OUTLAWED, ONLY OUTLAWS WILL BE MANLY

I T WAS AN image that set ten million pairs of trendy eyes rolling. I'm referring to the pictures from a few years back of George W. Bush in jeans, a straw Stetson, and leather work gloves clearing brush on his Crawford, Texas, ranch. Not since Ronald Reagan was photographed splitting firewood at Rancho Mirage have so many East Coast liberal gag reflexes been triggered en masse.

The instinct of the sophisticates was to declare it fake. Contrived. A pose for the cameras. The *Washington Post* headline chortled, "Down on the Ranch, President Wages War on the Underbrush."[1] *Vanity Fair* magazine, that widely recognized authority on all things farming and ranching, declared the brush clearing only "for show" and "completely unnecessary," while describing the ranch as "a perfect backdrop for his cowboy image."[2]

Of course, anyone well acquainted with the former president and who has spent time with him in Crawford knows that the *real* George Bush is the one you saw there in the dirty T-shirt with the chain saw. It is the guy we saw in a starched shirt with French cuffs at state dinners who wasn't totally at ease.

One suspects that what liberal cynics had such a powerful allergic reaction to in those photographs were the distinct traces of *testosterone*. From midtown Manhattan offices to Upper West Side apartments to Rodeo Drive designer boutiques to elite university Chomsky symposiums, you'll be hard-pressed to find anyone who has any use for manly men.

Now we have all lived to witness the ascendance of the "metrosexual." It's a term coined by writer Mark Simpson in an article in which he wrote:

Metrosexual man, the single young man with a high disposable income, living or working in the city (because that's where all the best shops are), is perhaps the most promising consumer market of the decade. In the eighties he was only to be found inside fashion magazines such as *GQ*, in television advertisements for Levis jeans or in gay bars. In the nineties, he's everywhere and he's going shopping.[3]

I just need to say it…I'm allergic to shopping!

Now that the term "metrosexual" has permeated the popular culture, you'll even find it in the *Oxford English Dictionary*, where the listing says:

n. A heterosexual man whose lifestyle, spending habits and concern for personal appearance are likened to those considered typical of a fashionable, urban, homosexual man.[4]

If, as some have suggested, the last few decades have witnessed a feminist-led "war on masculinity," then the rise of the metrosexual is surely evidence of our unconditional surrender. But the picture of American manhood is actually more complicated than that.

In typical dysfunctional fashion, though, while one large segment of America's men hurtled into a ditch on one side of the road, another went careening for the opposite culvert. Thus, we have the rise of the brute to parallel the rise of the snoot.

How else to explain the immense popularity of both *Queer Eye for the Straight Guy* and a growing variety of ultimate fighting and mixed martial arts programs focusing on the delicate art of cage fighting? Think about that term *cage fighting* for a moment. What are cages traditionally for? Animals, of course—wild, dangerous animals.

There you have the other ditch that popular culture would gladly push us into. Young men today are basically being offered two starkly different but both very twisted models of manhood. On the one hand, there is the waifish, delicate, ultrasensitive, hyper-groomed, body-waxed shopping buddy for his girlfriend. On the other is the tattooed, shaven-headed gladiator on a Darwinian quest to pass on his genes through as many women as possible. One is a tamed poodle, and the other is a snarling beast.

Both, by the way, are self-absorbed and obsessed with their own appearance. And neither is anywhere close to the God-intended blend of strength, gentleness, courage, and selflessness that makes for a great husband, an effective dad, and a victorious tamer of this wild and chaotic world.

That this dual-track dysfunction is emerging in manly identity shouldn't come as a surprise to us. For some time now, our "progressive" educational establishment, in conjunction with humanistic psychology professionals, has been sending the message to young boys that their very maleness is some kind of disorder that needs to be treated. If it's true that maleness is a disorder, I am happy to be thoroughly disordered. It started early. When I was a boy I had a matched pair of cap-gun six-shooters, a cowboy hat, blue jeans rolled up at the cuffs, a burr hair cut, and my big old Collie dog that made a great pony.... Relax, PETA; I was weight appropriate and I had no spurs.

Author Christina Hoff Sommers has documented our culture's peculiar opinion of what a man is in her eye-opening book entitled, *The War Against Boys: How Misguided Feminism Is Harming Our Young Men*.

Sommers's book is invariably described in the mainstream press as controversial. It's controversial only because it exposes a lot of hurtful feminist orthodoxy to the harsh light of fact. She introduces the work by writing:

> This book tells the story of how it has become fashionable to attribute pathology to millions of healthy male children. It is a story of how we are turning against boys and forgetting a simple truth: that the energy, competitiveness, and corporal daring of normal, decent males is responsible for much of what is right in the world. No one denies that boys' aggressive tendencies must be checked and channeled in constructive ways. Boys need discipline, respect, and moral guidance. Boys need love and tolerant understanding. They do not need to be pathologized.[5]

So, we start boys out by making them feel that much of what makes them male is somehow inappropriate or dysfunctional. But we allow them to be exposed to an avalanche of realistic violence and unhealthy sex through video games, television, movies, and computers. Is it any wonder why we have a shortage of men who know how to exhibit balanced, healthy masculinity?

Forty years ago, the old feminist orthodoxy was basically: "There are no inherent differences between men and women (other than a little plumbing). Any differences were purely the result of conditioning and environment." Today the new feminist orthodoxy boldly says, "Women are superior to men; boys and men should be feminized as much as possible."

So our culture presents the American male with a false dilemma: Be a manicured metrosexual or a tattooed cage fighter. Be a lot like a woman or a lot like an animal.

Somewhere in between those extremes is the higher, better way that is consistent with the Designer's plan. And I suspect there are a lot of women who would love to see more men expressing it.

SUMMARY (PART 3)

D O YOU REMEMBER that golden season when Cindy Sheehan and her traveling three-ring peace circus were camped down the road from President Bush's Crawford, Texas, ranch?

The media couldn't get enough of Ms. Sheehan back then. How giddy they were to have someone with moral authority and an aura of untouchability willing to voice loathing for President Bush and denounce the war.

To be fair, Ms. Sheehan had suffered a heartbreaking personal loss. Naturally, a steady stream of Hollywood Lefties capitalized on it. They made the pilgrimage to Crawford to be filmed standing next to Sheehan, usually in a T-shirt emblazoned with some too-clever antiwar slogan. (Please note: the sight of Ed Asner in a T-shirt is not for those with a weak constitution.)

Then Ms. Sheehan became a little too much of a good thing for those who were using her. In speeches and interviews, she started making some of the most incandescently silly statements ever uttered on a legitimate major newscast by someone not in handcuffs.

I have to confess to being a little amused watching the slow, horrified dawning of realization upon the mainstream media that Sheehan was a bit of a loon. She quickly became a liability to the cause of undermining Bush, and, for the most part, those with the cameras and microphones ever...so...slowly...backed...away.

I mention it because some of the signs I remember seeing at those Crawford photo ops stand out in my mind. Invariably, there were placards and banners shouting, "Bring Our Children Home" and "'Before One More Mother's Child Is Lost'—Cindy Sheehan."

It was and continues to be a common type of infantilization of adult fighting men and women that is different in character and in motive from the old World War II sentiment of "Let's support our *boys* in uniform." As was Sheehan's brave and honorable fallen son, Casey, every man and women wearing an American uniform today is a volunteer. They can vote, live on their own, marry, parent, and launch Internet ventures they can then sell for hundreds of millions of dollars.

In other words, they're not children.

Ironically, many of those who think nineteen- and twenty-year-olds aren't responsible for their enlistment decisions happen to also believe that twelve- and thirteen-year-olds have the same judgment and discernment as adults.

For example, to kick off the 2007 school year in Portland, Maine, school officials approved a plan to offer birth control prescriptions through their student health center. The step made King Middle School the first in Maine to make "a full range of contraception available to students in grades 6 through 8..."[1]

What is the compelling reason for a measure that now makes birth control pills available to eleven-year-old girls? What is the crisis? According to a news report: "Five of the 134 students [just under 4 percent] who visited King's health center during the 2006-07 school year reported having sexual intercourse," said Amanda Rowe, lead nurse in Portland's school health centers.[2]

In these two stories we see the Far Left's upside-down thinking in full-spectrum, living color. Grown volunteer soldiers are "our children"— note the collective pronoun there. Yet *actual* children are burdened with responsibility for grown-up choices and expectations about sex.

I suppose the only thing needed to completely round out the picture would be to throw in Howard Stern—a man in his mid-fifties who behaves like a juvenile and adds to the stream of untreated pornographic waste that flows into the popular culture and down to middle schoolers. The hat trick! In fact, pretty much every pathology already identified is embodied in Stern's life and actions. Now that I think about it, instead of writing the entire preceding section, I could have just shown you a photo of Stern and called it a day.

The question remains, where is true north in these matters?

First, where children are concerned, we're going to have to push back against the *our* children, collectivist mentality that permeates Washington DC and much of the rest of the culture. How? By putting parents back in the driver's seat where their kids are concerned.

Lots of parents have bought into the collectivist mentality, and understandably so. They've been told for decades by the schools and the government, "Trust us. We're the experts. We know what's best." Just last week my wife, Joni, reminded an educational specialist that he was an expert in his field of study but that, as our son's mother, she was the expert on the subject of her son! So many parents have allowed the popular culture to make them feel prudish or narrow-minded for objecting to the filth being peddled. Thus, too many moms and dads have been passive about and detached from what their kids are learning, watching, and hearing.

Parents must become fully engaged with their kids, not just academically but emotionally and socially too.

Robust, unapologetic parental engagement is essential, and nothing less will keep the culture from forcing children to grow up too soon.

And what about our growing ranks of what Diana West, in her book *The Death of the Grown-Up,* has called "perpetual adolescence?" Regarding the widespread tendency for thirty-five-year-old men to wince and take offense if someone addresses them as *sir,* she writes:

> "I'm not old enough to be a 'mister,'" goes the middle-aged refrain, a reflexive denial of the difference between old and young. The plaintive little protest is no throwaway line. Rather, it's a motto, even a prayer, that attests to our civilization's near-religious devotion to perpetual adolescence.[3]

Is it possible that many Americans are obsessed with seeming young because they're so terrified of growing old? I suspect it's no coincidence that the sharp rise in the cult of youth has paralleled a coinciding drop in belief in the Bible (and its promises of an afterlife). In other words, as our increasingly secular society begins to think this life may be "all there is," it becomes ever more desperate to hold on to youth as long as possible.

This generation's missing key to maturity in this life may very well be a simple confidence that something good can follow it. It seems C. S. Lewis had this very truth in mind when in *Mere Christianity* he wrote:

> If you read history you will find that the Christians who did the most for the present world were just those who thought most of the next.... It is since Christians have largely ceased to think of the other world that they have become so ineffective in this.[4]

Here in this world, we are facing pivotal, dangerous times—times filled with fierce challenges that Howard Stern, MTV's *Jackass*, and Adult Swim on the Cartoon Network leave our perpetual adolescents ill-equipped to meet.

PART 4

HEADSTANDS AND HEADS UP

OVERVIEW

IN AN ERA in which upside-down thinking is so prevalent, there are, unfortunately, hundreds of prominent, influential people spouting the most sublime nonsense on a regular basis. And they do it with the passion, conviction, and moral certitude of an eighteenth-century abolitionist preacher.

There are some telltale signs of standing-on-your-head thinking, and it is important to recognize them. There are, at the same time, reasoned voices from unexpected quarters. It is an easy thing to ascribe evil to one side and goodness to the other, but of course, heads-up thinking isn't always so simple. If we can begin to encourage the good we see, no matter where it exists, and discourage the errors we find, even if they are made by our friends, perhaps healing can begin.

With so many voices shouting at us from television, magazine pages, Web sites, and movie screens, a little discernment goes a long way. I've already pointed out much of the craziness and lunacy, but a few categories deserve separate mention. And with gratitude I will also single out a few of the courageous actions taken by some with worldviews distinctively different from mine.

HEADSTANDS

O H MY. IT takes a peculiar kind of skill to maintain the head-stands I am about to describe, but the acrobatic tricks can be witnessed day and night across our country.

AMERICA THE UN-GREAT

It's easy to spot the card-carrying members of the "Blame America First, Last, and Always" club. They tend to fawn over tinhorn dictators while characterizing (or *caricaturizing*) our nation's modest efforts to monitor the phone chat of international terrorists as the rise of a brutal police state. Any tragedy at any spot on the globe can be traced directly back to the good old U.S. of A. Of these folks, Michael Barone has noted:

> The default assumption predisposes them to believe that if there is slaughter in Darfur, it is our fault; if there are IEDs in Iraq, it is our fault; if peasants in Latin America are living in squalor, it is our fault; if there are climate changes that have any bad effect on anybody, it is our fault.[1]

A few months after 9/11, Columbia professor Todd Gitlin, an intellectually honest and courageous liberal, wrote (in the extreme Left *Mother Jones* magazine, of all places):

> [In] the wake of September 11 there erupted something more primal and reflexive than criticism: a kind of left-wing fundamentalism, a negative faith in America the ugly.
>
> In this cartoon view of the world, there is nothing worse than American power—not the woman-enslaving Taliban, not an unre-

pentant al Qaeda committed to killing civilians as they please—and America is nothing but a self-seeking bully.[2]

In this "cartoon view of the world," all the things that make America great are somehow viewed as unpardonable sins for which it must atone.

ABSOLUTES? ABSOLUTELY NOT

A second characteristic common to the behavior of upside-down individuals is the tendency to become utterly unhinged when encountering anyone holding moral values or making a moral argument. Keep in mind, we are living in a postmodern culture that has embraced, with absolute moral certainty, the idea that there is no such thing as absolute moral certainty. Thus, the one quality most likely to be held up for mockery and derision on fake news shows and late-night entertainment programs is *earnestness*.

Thus, fake news interviews are conducted with unsuspecting people who don't realize they're the butt of the joke. So, a little old lady is encouraged to prattle on and on for the camera about her prized yarn collection so that later, with some clever editing, her sincerity can trigger howls of laughter from urbane sophisticates.

Both comedian Sacha Baron Cohen (with his "Borat" character) and the MTV television program *Jackass* are wildly successful with younger audiences. Both have gotten lots of mileage out of the same shtick. One of the most popular pranks perpetrated by the *Jackass* crew (was there ever a more appropriate name for a television program?) involved placing an infant car-seat type carrier containing a life-sized doll on top of a car in a busy parking lot and then waiting. The car would begin to drive off as hidden cameras captured the efforts of horrified good Samaritans running after the vehicle, waving their arms and shouting for it to stop.

Nothing says *comedy* like making good people think a baby is about to be injured or killed and then goofing on their frantic efforts to help. Suckers are hilarious.

Whether it comes from the Left or the Right, from a Christian or a

Christian Scientist, what the popular culture finds most unacceptable is simple confidence that a certain thing is true. To assert in a public debate that a certain policy would be wrong is now seen as trying to "shove your morality down someone else's throat."

THE BABY AND THE BATHWATER

Another way to spot a person truly worthy of the Headstand Hall of Fame is to recognize in them the overwhelming tendency to impute bad faith and bad motives to anyone who disagrees with them.

A person is never simply wrong; instead, he is a moron. Others don't hold different opinions or differing values; they're "worse than Hitler." Headstanders have no need to try to understand any contrary viewpoint—the holders are simply "stupid, crazy, evil, or all of the above." They seem to find it easy to not only dismiss differing viewpoints but to also dismiss the human value of those who hold them.

If someone expresses concern for the unborn from a human rights and civil rights standpoint, they're told that they *really* are only interested in keeping women in their barefoot-and-pregnant place.

If you oppose federal welfare programs on the grounds that they lead to dependency, undermine the family structure, and have other unintended negative consequences, you're told that your *real* reasons are nothing more than greed and coldheartedness.

When you express concern that redefining marriage to include same-sex couples will put the culture on a slippery slope toward the complete dissolution of the family structure, carrying with it disastrous long-term effects for our nation, you will be told that in actuality you suffer from a mental pathology, a form of psychosis called *homophobia*.

And former President Bush wasn't misinformed by flawed intelligence about Iraq's weapons of mass destruction. He "lied and people died." It was all about oil. Except that it was *really* all about revenge for Saddam's attempted assassination of his father. Strike that. It was *actually* about construction contracts for Halliburton. No, wait. It was a Zionist conspiracy hatched by Israeli intelligence. It was anything—*anything*—

but a straightforward policy decision sincerely made in the best interests of the nation using the best information available at the time.

G. K. Chesterton once observed that, "In a world in which everything is ridiculous, nothing can be ridiculed."[3] Instead, shouldn't we point out the ridiculous when we see it? Should we speak up in response to:

- The blatantly propagandist film that isn't really intended to win over the other side or even persuade the neutral. Its sole purpose is to rev up the true believers, fill them with a burning sense of their own righteousness, and demonize the enemy, with no attempt to be truthful, accurate, or fair.

- The ratings-driven talk show host who can't seem to quit ranting about religion or pointing fingers at one political side or the other, without real facts or honest discussion

- The cartoonist whose work drips with condescension and loathing for Middle America and her values along with deep disdain for men and women who volunteer for military service

- The persistent conspiracy theorists who promote astoundingly implausible lies regarding some of America's most sensitive issues, including the "Truther" movement that insists America was actually behind the attacks of 9/11. (Let that sink in and then join me in weeping for our nation.) Additional "cults" include those who have convinced themselves that Sarah Palin's youngest child, Trig, is not really her baby at all and the theorists known as "birthers," who doubt the authenticity of President Barack Obama's birth certificate.

- Angry Internet commenters who, while safely hiding behind their chat-room aliases, feel free to say things they know would get them punched in the nose if they were face-to-face with their audience. In this world, plenty of bile and bad will flow from every direction. As Stanley Kurtz, a Senior Fellow at the Ethics and Public Policy Center, observed a while back: "Our political anger is only the most impressive expression of a much wider cultural transformation. In politics, in music, in sports, on the Web, in our families, and in the relations between the sexes, American anger has come into its own."[4]

How sad for us. How upside down.

But all is not darkness and despair. Sometimes hope comes from unexpected quarters.

30

HEADS UP

I'T'S BEEN MY unpleasant but necessary duty to be your guide on this tour of America's dangerous experiment with upside-down thinking. Along the way we've seen scores of examples of the destructive tendency to call wrong, right... ugly, lovely... and the ridiculous, sublime.

Here at the end of such a tour I would be remiss if I didn't focus the spotlight on a few examples of refreshingly right-side-up thinking. Frankly, in a culture such as ours, it takes courage and a thick skin to swim—even for a moment—against the furious tide of backward self-deception. Thankfully, amid our dark epidemic of Younger Bear Syndrome it is possible to locate flashes of healthy head-pointing-toward-the-sky thinking. They ought to be commended wherever we find them, but especially when they appear in the perverse realms of media, politics, entertainment, or academia.

Here are a few noteworthy examples.

CHRIS MATTHEWS

The MSNBC network began as a typical left-leaning news outlet but has lurched even farther leftward with breathtaking haste in recent years. With an on-air staff of opinion-driven show hosts like Keith Olbermann, Rachel Maddow, and Ed Schulz, as well as "straight news" reporters like Andrea Mitchell and David Shuster,[1] who long ago stopped trying to hide their political sympathies, the network's brand has become synonymous with vitriolic attacks on conservatives, Republicans, and evangelical

Christians, not to mention daily attacks on their more conservative, more successful rival, FOX News Channel.

In the center ring of this media circus sits Chris Matthews and his program called *Hardball*.

Matthews is no conservative. In fact, he consistently provokes the ire of Republicans with his left-leaning political commentary and loaded questions for his conservative guests. During the presidential election of 2008, he famously mentioned that a speech by candidate Obama had caused a "thrill to run up his leg."[2] Matthews briefly considered a run, as a Democrat, for the Pennsylvania Senate seat held by Arlen Specter, before Specter switched parties.

Like most of the New York/Washington broadcast news establishment, Matthews is a liberal Democrat. But it might surprise some conservatives to learn that he is frequently the target of harsh, sometimes vicious, criticism from the Left. What earns him these attacks is a stubborn streak of intellectual honesty and occasional nostalgic spasms of something that is increasingly rare among mainstream news media types—old school journalistic ethics.

For example, in the heat of the 2008 elections when much of the press corps had early on become little more than cheerleaders for the Obama campaign (much to the dismay of Hillary Clinton and her husband), Matthews grilled an Obama supporter, a state senator from Texas, and ultimately forced him to admit that he couldn't name a single legislative accomplishment by the senator from Illinois. The widely discussed embarrassment for the Obama campaign did not win Matthews many brownie points on the Left. Indeed, the *Hardball* host frequently gets called out by the liberal, George Soros–funded Media Matters Web site, bloggers for the Daily Kos, and writers for the *Huffington Post* for straying from left-wing talking points.

In a shining moment of contrarian courage when he was a guest panelist on Bill Maher's *Real Time* HBO program, Matthews rebuked Maher's long, bizarre, self-indulgent rant about vaccinations being potentially dangerous. When Matthews had heard enough, he interrupted Maher, saying, "What are you talking about? . . . Why are you doing this, why are you fighting this fight?...You sound like Tom Cruise saying 'I don't believe in therapy.'"[3]

On Maher's show, as on his own, Chris Matthews said precisely what he thinks, regardless of whom and which side his words will annoy. In our increasingly biased media that's a commendable and often entertaining quality.

BART STUPAK

In the nation's long and tortuous battle over health care legislation that raged throughout 2009 and 2010, a number of courageous pro-life Democrats in the House of Representatives stood resolute in the face of bone-crushing pressure to compromise their convictions. Especially noteworthy was their primary spokesman and leader, Michigan congressman Bart Stupak.

Representative Stupak lent his name to an amendment to the House version of the legislation that guaranteed that the long-standing ban on using federal dollars to pay for abortions would be maintained under the new system of government mandates for health insurance providers and subsidies for health insurance purchasers. With the help of a handful of fellow Democrats and most of the House Republicans, Stupak got his amendment passed in spite of withering criticism and threats of retribution from the pro-abortion majority within his own caucus.

Stupak had to face another tsunami of pressure to abandon his pro-life principles when, in March of 2010, House Speaker Nancy Pelosi and Senate Majority Leader Harry Reid tried to get the Senate version of the bill passed through a parliamentary maneuver called *reconciliation*. The Senate version of the bill had no pro-life protections against federal funding for abortion. In fact, it explicitly called for such funding.

On March 12, 2010, Stupak told a conservative news magazine that he and his fellow pro-life Dems were coming under "enormous" political pressure from both the White House and House Speaker. "I am a definite 'no' vote," he told the reporter:

"We're all getting pounded by our traditional Democratic supporters, like unions.... This has really reached an unhealthy stage," Stupak says. "People are threatening ethics complaints on me. On the Left, they're really stepping it up. Every day, from Rachel Maddow to the *Daily Kos*, it keeps coming. Does it bother me? Sure. Does it change my position? No."[4]

Yes, I know. He eventually acquiesced and voted for the bill while getting virtually nothing in exchange. However, for a few shining moments, he held the line for life. In the upside-down world of Washington where political survival is the highest value, political courage is a rare thing to behold even if it is temporary.

GARY SINISE

As noted in previous chapters, the default setting in Hollywood is to paint the U.S. military as either psychopaths or dullards. It sometimes seems that the fastest track to having your movie project "green lit" is to make sure it portrays our men and women in uniform or those in our intelligence services as buffoons or criminals or, optimally, both. How else does one explain George Clooney's spectacular flop *The Men Who Stare at Goats*?

I could fill the next several pages with titles of movies made in the last decade that follow this tired formula.

Against this backdrop comes a breath of fresh air named Gary Sinise, a successful and talented actor who brilliantly played Lt. Dan Taylor, a Vietnam veteran and double-amputee in 1994's *Forrest Gump*. Sinise also has a long-running role as the lead character on *CSI: NY*.

Going all the way back to the early days of the conflicts in Afghanistan and Iraq—when most of the usual suspects in Hollywood (paging Sean Penn) were making their usual comments—Sinise was encouraging unwavering, unqualified support for our military personnel, regardless of what one thought about their assignments. "It's very important that we give back to these volunteers who serve our nation because they're on the front lines for us, and they need to know we care," Sinise told a reporter.

"Perhaps one of the reasons that I've jumped on board so strongly for the USO, and for supporting the service members in this time of war, is that I do remember how our Vietnam veterans were treated when they came home, and we can never let that happen again."[5]

According to the USA Patriotism! Web site, he once told the *Chicago Sun-Times*, "I think we do owe our troops a huge debt of gratitude for the sacrifices they make. This is an all-volunteer service, and they're around the world defending our country or helping others defend themselves."[6] The fact is, Sinise has become Tinseltown's most vocal and consistent advocate for support of our military personnel.

The actor has done more than talk, however. He's put his time and money where his mouth is. He's been a one-man throwback to the Hollywood era of World War II in which actors could be counted on to do their part to boost morale (or at least not actively work to undermine it).

Sinise formed a rock band called the Lt. Dan Band, in which he plays bass guitar. The band plays benefit concerts to raise money for causes such as the Wounded Warrior Fund and has entertained the troops in Iraq and Afghanistan on numerous occasions.[7] After a trip to Iraq exposed Sinise to the role U.S. soldiers were playing in helping build and restore Iraqi schools, he formed Operation Iraqi Children (since renamed Operation International Children) to support and augment our efforts in Iraq and elsewhere.[8]

In December 2008 the actor received the Presidential Citizen Medal, the second-highest honor that can be awarded a U.S. civilian. He received the medal for his humanitarian contributions to Iraqi school children and his involvement in the USO.

All the while, Sinise has been boldly bucking another fashionable Hollywood trend. He has been married to the same woman for thirty years.

MIA FARROW

In the entertainment world, popular causes come and go. One week the *cause du jour* might be wind power; the next, sea otters. When a natural disaster strikes, a good number of celebrities can be counted on to show up at an event and raise some money. A few will even take the time to visit the disaster site and raise awareness of the need. All this is commendable to the degree that it does some good. But what is rare among the beautiful people is a long-term, sacrificial commitment to a truly worthy cause. And that is what makes Mia Farrow stand out.

As I mentioned in chapter 17, Hollywood came late to an awareness of a holocaust in Darfur, but better late than never. Now most have moved on to the next big thing. Mia Farrow, on the other hand, came early, has stayed late, and has gotten her hands dirty.

As a UNICEF goodwill ambassador, Farrow has worked to draw attention to the fight to eradicate polio—a disease she survived as a child and that is making a comeback in several parts of the world. She has traveled to Darfur numerous times to advocate for Darfuri refuges.[9] She has also been actively involved in addressing appalling humanitarian and human rights tragedies in Chad, Uganda, and the Congo. Her photographs of Darfur have been published in newspapers around the world and in *People* magazine. She has penned moving editorials that have appeared in the *Wall Street Journal* and many other online sites and blogs.[10]

Farrow consistently displays a brand of deep, sacrificial passion for her cause that is usually only witnessed in missionaries. For example, in August of 2007 Farrow offered to "trade her freedom" for the freedom of a Sudanese rebel leader who had taken refuge in a UN hospital and was afraid to leave for fear of being assassinated or imprisoned by the Sudanese government. She offered herself as a hostage in exchange for him being allowed to leave the country.[11]

In March of 2009, the International Criminal Court issued a warrant for the arrest of Sudanese President Omar al-Bashir and, in retaliation, the government there expelled thirteen international aid agencies from Darfur. To draw attention to this humanitarian travesty, Farrow began a water-only fast.[12] Her goal was to fast for three weeks, but after twelve days she was forced to call a halt to the fast due to rapid deterioration of her health.[13]

In recent years, Farrow has been involved with the Dream for Darfur campaign, which has done us all a great service by focusing public attention on China's unconscionable support for the government of Sudan. Her efforts resulted in Steven Spielberg's last-minute withdrawal as an artistic advisor to the Chinese government for the 2008 Summer Olympics in Beijing.[14] During those games, Farrow hosted a series of Internet broadcasts from a Sudanese refugee camp to highlight China's catastrophic involvement in the region.[15]

On top of all that, in 2009, the actress agreed to narrate a documentary film called *As We Forgive*, which documents the struggle of many of the survivors of the Rwandan genocide to come to a place of forgiveness toward those who murdered their fathers, mothers, sisters, brothers, children, and friends.[16]

In 2008, the organization Refugees International awarded Farrow their "McCall-Pierpaoli Humanitarian Award for extraordinary service to refugees and displaced people."[17]

I say it was well deserved.

CHRISTOPHER HITCHENS

Could a Bible-waving, flyover state country gospel preacher like me have some words of commendation for one of the world's most vocal proponents of atheism? Yes, indeed.

Christopher Hitchens, author of *God Is Not Great: How Religion Poisons Everything*, may be dead wrong about the existence of a loving Creator. But he is spot-on when it comes to warning America and the West about the dangers of Islamic extremism and creeping Sharia.

Hitchens was and is a man of the radical Left, with a long history of involvement in advocacy of socialist causes. The British writer is also the most visible advocates for a new and rising brand of militant atheism. A self-described "anti-theist," you'll frequently find him arguing the no-God side in high-profile debates.

But after the 9/11 attacks on America in 2001, Hitchens became something else as well. Much to the consternation of his fellow liberals, he became a powerful and articulate defender of America's muscular response to the growing threat of terrorism fueled by extreme manifestations of radical Islam. The blame-America-first crowd that had grown accustomed to having Hitchens's sharp wit and even sharper tongue arguing for their side now found themselves on the receiving end of his barbs.

For example, Hitchens had been a regular feature on the pages of the Far Left magazine *The Nation* for decades. But about a year after the 9/11 attacks, he very vocally parted company with the publication, ending his regular "Minority Report" column by writing that *The Nation*...

> ... is becoming the voice and the echo chamber of those who truly believe that John Ashcroft is a greater menace than Osama bin Laden. (I too am resolutely opposed to secret imprisonment and terror-hysteria, but not in the same way as I am opposed to those who initiated the aggression, and who are planning future ones.) In these circumstances it seems to me false to continue the association, which is why I have decided to make this "Minority Report" my last one.[18]

Over the next eight years, Hitchens became more than an advocate for military action in Afghanistan and Iraq. He was a scathing critic of the apologists for terrorists and of those in the United States and Europe who seemed so eager to sacrifice our freedoms and our cultural traditions in the cause of appeasing intolerant extremists.

Hitchens won a lifetime of good will from conservatives on a single night when the writer was a guest on Bill Maher's HBO program, *Real Time*.

The obnoxious Maher, who is himself a militant atheist and has co-produced a movie mocking religious people, might have expected to find a kindred spirit in Hitchens. But when, in the middle of a discussion about Iran and its loony leader, Mahmoud Ahmadinejad, Maher made a typically ludicrous statement suggesting that President Bush was a greater threat to world security than the Iranian despot, Hitchens squashed the assertion like a bug.

> Who wants a Third World War? The Iranian President says that one member state of the United Nations should be wiped physically from

the map with all its people. He says the United States is a Satanic power. Members of his government, named members of his government have been caught sponsoring deaths [*sic*] squads. He's lied, he's lied to the European Union about his nuclear program....He says the Messiah is about to come back. Who's looking for a war here?[19]

To this, Maher came back with a lame joke about President Bush expecting the Messiah too. This elicited the usual Pavlovian hoots, claps, and cheers from Maher's boorish audience. "I'm not being facetious here," Maher quickly added.[20]

To which Hitchens replied, "That's not facetious. But your audience, which will clap at apparently anything, is frivolous."[21]

That sparked a round of groans and boos from the crowd, which Hitchens calmly acknowledged with a common salute that utilized a single finger on his right hand.

Profane? Indeed. Refreshingly cathartic for anyone who has ever had to suffer through one of Maher's programs? You bet. More importantly, it demonstrates that in Christopher Hitchens—who became a U.S. citizen on the steps of the Jefferson Memorial on his fifty-eighth birthday in 2007—America has an articulate and unabashed advocate for the advancement of freedom and democracy around the world.

There are many others I could cite for commendation in this section. But this handful of examples should suffice to show that there is indeed cause for hope in the struggle to right our inverted culture. That hope, and the reasons for it, is what we explore in the concluding pages that follow.

RIGHTING A "CONTRARY" CULTURE

W E'RE LIVING ON our heads.
Like a whole tribe of Younger Bears from *Little Big Man*,
we've become a collection of "Contraries"—thinking,
believing, and acting precisely backward in so many vital areas.

After the journey we've taken together through these pages, it would
be difficult to come to any other conclusion. And yet my aim in being
your friendly tour guide through Bizarro World wasn't merely to share
outrages and absurdities so we could shake our heads, shrug our shoulders, and maybe laugh or cry a little together.

I've gone to the trouble of pointing out many of the ways in which
our culture's thinking is upside down only because I'm convinced it can
be righted. Yes, believe it or not, in spite of the litany of confusion and
contrariness I've catalogued—in the face of a society with large segments
of people who have convinced themselves that good men are monsters,
life is bad, killing is a virtue, and children and adults should switch
places—I'm genuinely hopeful!

I know I've been tough in these pages on those who represent the
most extreme manifestations of upside-down thinking in our nation.
And appropriately so, I think. But if you'll read other things I've written
or come visit the church I pastor, you'll discover I'm much, much tougher
on my fellow Christians and the church!

Although the extremists I've highlighted here are influential and
powerful, they don't represent the vast, commonsensical middle of American society. I've also come to understand that the folks in the middle are

weary of Red State versus Blue State polarization and yearn for principled solutions to our deepest problems. They're tired of being continually
reminded of what divides us; they would welcome some attention to and
celebration of those things that unite us.

What kinds of things?

Parents, be they Republican or Democrat, love their kids desperately
and want to see them safe, healthy, and ultimately raised to be productive, functional, happy adults. I don't know any parent who is not at least
a little concerned about what the ubiquity of Myspace and Facebook
and text messaging will mean for the emotional and social well-being of
their children.

No one wants to be a victim of crime. Everyone appreciates clean
water to drink and clean air to breathe. And only the most twisted
among us hope to see another major terrorist attack on our shores. A
large majority of us think the term *marriage* should mean something
specific—and know that if it can be made to mean *anything*, then it will
quickly mean *nothing*.

These and many other things represent common ground.

Lately Newt Gingrich has been saying some great things along these
very lines. As chairman of a group called American Solutions for
Winning the Future, Gingrich has come up with something he calls a
"Platform for the American People." It is an effort to make progress on
some key items that a large majority of us agree about. In an op-ed in the
Des Moines Register, Gingrich wrote:

> For example, by a margin of 87 percent to 11 percent, Americans
> believe English should be the official language of government. Vast
> majorities of Democrats, Republicans, and independents agree. The
> majority of Hispanic Americans agree.
>
> Extensive polling research shows extraordinary unity among
> Americans on the core issues and values that define us as a nation.
> For instance, 95 percent of us believe we have the obligation to be
> good stewards of God's creation.
>
> Ninety-three percent believe al Qaeda poses a serious threat to
> our nation. Ninety-six percent believe it's important for the president

and Congress to address the problem of Social Security in the next few years.[1]

Of course, to successfully bridge the political and ideological chasms that currently divide us so we can come together on these common-values issues, we're going to have to find a way to turn down the volume on what passes for public discourse in this country. The profanity-enriched bile that pours forth on the comment threads of most political blogs and Web sites, the shout-fests on talk radio, and the shtick of labeling good people "The Worst Person in the World" must stop; and if not, then somehow it must be tuned out.

I think both the *New York Times*'s Frank Rich *and* my friend Ann Coulter (with whom I agree a great deal of the time) need to ratchet down the rhetoric a few notches, even if doing so curtails the red meat diet of the roaring lions on their respective ends of the political spectrum. Those lions are overfed anyway.

We're going to have to find a way to spark a renaissance of good faith and good will, and I believe we can.

That doesn't mean, however, that we can turn a blind eye to these key areas in which the thinking and values of many have become inverted. It *does* mean that our aim should be to persuade and win over—rather than condemn and shame. The latter is easy and gratifies our lowest instincts. The former takes hard work and forces us to draw upon our better angels.

There is work to be done in each of the realms represented by the first three sections in this book. For example, we need to rediscover what real good guys look like and celebrate real heroism when we see it. However and wherever the long, difficult war on global terrorism proceeds, we need to make sure our servicemen and servicewomen feel the kind of esteem and appreciation that was virtually universal in World War II.

As I have pointed out at numerous points throughout this book, there are too many places in America in which military service is clearly and wrongly viewed as low and ugly—fit only for the dense and the desperate.

Here's a start. Let's threaten to cut off federal funds, aid, and research grants to colleges that bar military recruiters from operating on campus, just as we do to Christian colleges if they fail to follow feminist Title IX guidelines in their athletic programs.

Let's shine a spotlight on places like Berkeley, California, where some citizens are still traumatized by the horror of having their liberal paradise soiled by the presence of the Marine Corps recruiting office that opened a few years back. In response, the city considered placing zoning restrictions on military recruiting offices, similar to the ones many communities use to limit the spread of X-rated businesses.

The Daily Californian reported:

> "In the same way that many communities limit the location of pornographic stores, that's the same way we feel about the military recruiting stations," said PhoeBe Sorgen, an initiative proponent and a member of the city's Peace and Justice Commission. "Teenagers that really want to find them will be able to seek them out and find them, but we don't want them in our face."[2]

The local attorney who drafted the measure—oops! I used the word *drafted*. Hope I didn't frighten anyone in Berkeley. I'll rephrase that—the local attorney who *wrote* the measure, Sharon Adams, said: "We feel that as a community we need to protect the youth. We're trying to level the playing field."[3]

Of course, a level playing field is what currently exists in Berkeley, where the Marines, a nail salon, and a feminist bookstore all have equal access to any available slot in a strip of storefronts. But no, in true Orwellian doublespeak fashion, when Ms. Adams talks about leveling playing fields, she means precisely the opposite. It is most telling that she and her like-minded Berkeleyans view the impulse to serve one's country as a temptation from which young people should be shielded at all costs.

The city councilwoman whose district is currently being defiled by the offending office said, "I do want to do something, whatever we can do, to shut down an agency that offends our public standards. It's a detriment. It's a danger to the public."[4]

And there you have it. The basic premise of this entire book captured in one glorious, neon, flaming, all-singing, all-dancing, upside-down example. The leading lights of Berkeley consider the presence of a Marine recruitment office a danger to the public and want to treat it the way most communities treat pornographic bookstores and strip clubs. (By the way, the city of Berkeley has no problem whatsoever with pornographic bookstores. Put one wherever you please.)

To add to the general sense of welcome and appreciation the Marines assigned to the Berkeley office must be feeling, the radical antiwar organization Code Pink has staged demonstrations in front of the recruitment center every Wednesday since it opened. But don't fret. I'm sure those good-natured gals from Code Pink show those Marines every bit of the courtesy and thanks they showed General David Petraeus during his testimony before Congress back in September of 2007.

What else can we do to right this capsized vessel of a culture? For one thing, the quiet majority of us who know that America is truly *good* (not perfect, but fundamentally good and a major force for good in the world) can be more vocal. With civility yet firmness we need to confront the new crop of blame-America-firsters about the obscenity of cozying up to dictators and despots while unfairly smearing our own great nation. (Danny Glover, call your office.)

On matters of life and death, we need to become skilled advocates for a culture of life. I loved the soft-focus, pro-adoption public service spots developed by the Arthur S. Demoss Foundation a generation ago, each of which ended with the tag line, "Life—What a Beautiful Choice." Now, in the age of YouTube and ubiquitous viral media, we need a new generation of creative types and philanthropists who will work together to open a new generation's eyes to the value and uniqueness of human life.

If a short home video of a baby laughing hysterically at his father can trigger more than 35 million views on YouTube, imagine what we can do in that medium to subtly but powerfully make the case that human life is precious and worthy of extraordinary protection.

Certainly we must throw ourselves in front of the rolling cultural forces that would sexualize our children, pressuring them to grow up far too fast—and shout, "Stop!" And if Justin Timberlake can "bring sexy back," maybe we can work together to bring adulthood back. And while we're at it, we can stop making masculine gentlemen feel like freakish throwbacks to the Ward Cleaver era for refusing to choose either the way of the tattooed cage fighter or the primped, coiffed metrosexual.

Certainly any and all of these steps would be a great start toward putting our bottoms-up nation right again. But there is one irreplaceable element that is more significant than any other.

We must set a place at the conference table for God.

The fact is, without Him, we are lost. By that I mean, if we allow the Word or witness of the Judeo-Christian God of the Bible to be declared out of bounds in our discussions, then there is no long-term healing possible for us.

Now don't tune me out just because I used the "*G* word." You've walked this far on this journey with me. Hang in just a little longer and I'll explain what I mean.

I mentioned at the opening of this conclusion that I'm hopeful about our chances of turning things around. There is a reason for that hope. You see, we've done it before. We've snapped out of a self-induced stupor of deception and put things right.

After two hundred years of rationalizing slavery and making excuses for its defiling presence on our shores, what can only be described as an awakening swept our land and compelled us to do the right thing.

That awakening began in America's pulpits. Preaching and Bible teaching stoked the fires of abolition. The ironclad intellectual framework for the case against slavery was forged not in city halls, but in prayer halls.

One hundred years later, when it was clear that the promise of equality for all people—the essential promise forged in the Declaration of Independence—was still not fully realized, it was pulpits and preachers and principled people who knew their Bibles who served as both the backbone and the heart of the civil rights movement.

And if we think we can now snap out of the deceptions and delusions that threaten our very existence as a nation without those very same assets, we're even more deceived than I think we are.

Secular, post-Christian Europe is defenseless against creeping Islami-fication, just as we will be if people of the historic Christian faith are declared ineligible to participate in the vital conversation we need to have *together*.

Why is it even necessary to make this point or issue such a warning? Because there is a new, militant strain of atheism spreading like a virus among the elites of academia and media. Bill Maher has a somewhat severe case of it. So do the reporters who like to ask Christian candidates for office whether they believe that every word of Genesis is literally true in hopes of getting them to say something that smug rationalists can hold up to ridicule. The entertainment duo, Penn & Teller, have it bad, as well. Their symptoms are on full display in their profanely named Show-time series (the show's name is a term for bovine manure followed by an exclamation point.) The show's Web page tells us:

> By their own admission, Penn & Teller have been dying to do a show like this. Confirmed skeptics and pro-science atheists (they refer to God as "an imaginary friend"), these magicians are big fans of the art of debunking.[5]

But as the above quote suggests, the old live-and-let-live brand of atheism is being shoved aside as a new militant strain emerges—one that is loud, abusive, and oddly evangelistic.

The main carriers of this contagion are a wave of books (*God Is Not Great, The God Delusion,* and *Breaking the Spell,* among others) that not only train virtual fire hoses of skepticism on religious experience in general and Christianity in particular but also actively promote aggres-sive intolerance of people of faith.

One of the worst of the bunch is a book called *The End of Faith* by Sam Harris. In this shrill and childish little tome, Harris declares, "…we must find our way to a time when faith, without evidence, disgraces anyone who would claim it."[6] But he's just getting warmed up. Later Harris writes a paragraph that the brilliant Theodore Dalrymple, a former "neo-atheist" himself, described as "quite possibly the most disgraceful thing that I have read in a book by a man posing as a ratio-nalist."[7] He was referring to these shocking words from Harris:

> The link between belief and behavior raises the stakes considerably. Some propositions are so dangerous that it may even be ethical to kill people for believing them. This may seem an extraordinary claim, but it merely enunciates an ordinary fact about the world in which we live.[8]

Here we have the logic of secular rationalism extended to its endpoint. People of faith are irrational. Irrational people are dangerous. It's ethical to kill dangerous people. People of faith may have to be killed.

Have a nice day!

Don't misunderstand. I'm not concerned that Harris's ideas will win the day and Christians will be wiped out. Sorry, that's been tried many times before, and it never works out. The vine of the Christian faith thrives in the hothouse of persecution.

No, my concern is that a nation of people will have lived so long on their heads that they might buy in to such madness. The church will go on. But such a nation is destined to fade into obscurity by way of absurdity.

Our nation—yours and mine.

Let's come together in the middle and set it right.

NOTES

Introduction
A Culture of "Contraries"

1. Joel Roberts, "Senator Reid on Iraq: 'This War Is Lost,'" CBS News, April 20, 2007, http://www.cbsnews.com/stories/2007/04/20/politics/main2709229.shtml (accessed April 28, 2010).

2. Howard Kurtz, "Trading the Talk for the Walk?" *Washington Post*, December 5, 2008, http://www.washingtonpost.com/wp-dyn/content/article/2008/12/04/AR2008120403901.html (accessed April 20, 2010).

3. Marcella Bombardieri, "Summers' Remarks on Women Draw Fire," *Boston Globe*, January 17, 2005, http://www.boston.com/news/local/articles/2005/01/17/summers_remarks_on_women_draw_fire/ (accessed April 21, 2010).

4. Scott Rasmussen, "Comedian Colbert Reaches Double Digits as Third-Party Candidate," *Rasmussen Reports*, October 24, 2007, http://www.rasmussenreports.com/public_content/politics/election_2008__1/2008_presidential_election/comedian_colbert_reaches_double_digits_as_third_party_candidate (accessed May 1, 2010).

5. David McNair, "Celebrity Culture in America," *Oldspeak: An Online Journal Devoted to Intellectual Freedom,* November 11, 2003, http://www.rutherford.org/Oldspeak/Articles/Art/oldspeak-celebrity2.asp (accessed May 1, 2010).

6. Thomas Hargrove, "Third of Americans Suspect 9-11 Government Conspiracy," Scripps News, August 1, 2006, http://www.scrippsnews.com/911poll (accessed May 1, 2010).

7. George Orwell, *1984* (New York: Penguin Group, 2003), 16.

8. Isaiah 5:20.

Part 1 Overview

1. Daniel J. Flynn, *Why the Left Hates America: Exposing the Lies That Have Obscured Our Nation's Greatness* (New York: Three Rivers Press, 2002, 2004), 3.

2. Ward Churchill, "'Some People Push Back': On the Justice of Roosting Chickens," Kersplebedeb.com, http://www.kersplebedeb.com/mystuff/s11/churchill.html (accessed April 28, 2010).

3. Ibid.

Chapter 1
Fawning Over Thugs

1. TheFreeDictionary.com, s.v. "Armando Valladares," http://encyclopedia.thefreedictionary.com/Armando+Valladares (accessed April 28, 2010).

2. R. Emmet Tyrell Jr., "Castro Shuffling in Place," CNN.com, http://www.cnn.com/2007/POLITICS/01/19/tyrrell.castro/index.html?iref=newssearch (accessed May 1, 2010).

3. Ibid.

4. Marc Morano, "Critics Assail Castro's 'Sickening' Grip on Hollywood Celebs," FrontPageMag.com, http://97.74.65.51/readArticle.aspx?ARTID=20515 (accessed April 28, 2010).

5. Ibid.

6. Eric Margolis, "Remembering Ukraine's Unknown Holocaust," The Wisdom Fund, http://www.twf.org/News/Y1998/19981213-UkraineHolocaust.html (accessed May 2, 2010).

7. Several pages of Soviet defector Victor Kravchenko's book *I Chose Freedom* were dedicated to American intellectuals. He was "shocked" when he realized that "Stalin's grip on the American mind...was almost as firm as his grip on the Russian mind." He describes how he had "to listen in frustrated silence" while American intellectuals spent hours praising Stalin's achievements. His endeavors to explain that this "tinselly picture of a happy and successful 'socialist' nation [was] imposed upon [the American] mind...by the best propaganda machine in all history" were useless. He found it "truly extraordinary" that "the Communist reality—like slave labour, police dictatorship, the massive periodic purges, the fantastically low standard of living, the great famine of 1932-33, the horrors of collectivization, the state organized child labor— seemed to have completely escaped American attention." Kravchenko relates that when he dared to mention such things to American intellectuals, they usually "looked at me incredulously and some even hastened to enter cocksure denials." Those who already knew about these atrocities readily tolerated them "as a kind of interlude before paradise is ushered in." Ivan Pongracic, "Learning From Experience," December 1993, Vol. 43, Issue 12, Foundation for Economic Education, http://www.fee.org/publications/the -freeman/article.asp?aid=2395 (accessed May 2, 2010).

8. "The Mugabe administration has been criticised around the world for corruption, suppression of political opposition, mishandling of land reform, economic mismanagement, and deteriorating human rights in Zimbabwe. According to most analysts his administration's policies have led to economic collapse and massive starvation over the course of the last ten years. Zimbabwe has the highest inflation rate in the world, predicted to hit 1.5 million percent by the end of 2007, and is, according to the United Nations Economic Commission for Africa, Africa's worst economic performer." Search.com, s.v. "Robert Mugabe," http://www.search.com/reference/ Robert_Mugabe (accessed April 28, 2010).

CHAPTER 2
DISHONORING OUR HEROES

1. Wikipedia.com, s.v. "Westboro Baptist Church," http://en.wikipedia.org/wiki/ Westboro_Baptist_Church#Claiming_divine_vengeance (accessed April 22, 2010).

2. Southern Poverty Law Center, "Fred Phelps Timeline," http://www.splcenter.org/ intel/intelreport/article.jsp?sid=184 (accessed May 2, 2010).

3. Westboro Baptist Church Web site, GodHatesFags.com, and http://www.sign movies.net/videos/signmovies/index.html (accessed April 22, 2010).

4. Ibid., http://www.godhatesfags.com.

5. Wikipedia.com, s.v. "Fred Phelps," http://en.wikipedia.org/wiki/Fred_Phelps (accessed May 2, 2010).

6. Shirley Phelps Roper, interview by Sean Hannity, *Hannity & Colmes*, April 18, 2006, http://media.pfaw.org/Right/PhelpsInterview.txt (accessed May 10, 2010).

7. The official Web site for the Patriot Guard Riders states: "Our main mission is to attend the funeral services of fallen American heroes *as invited guests of the family*. Each mission we undertake has two basic objectives. 1. Show our sincere respect for our fallen heroes, their families, and their communities. 2. Shield the mourning family and their friends from interruptions created by any protestor or group of protestors. We accomplish the latter through strictly legal and non-violent means." "Patriot Guard Riders Mission Statement," http://www.patriotguard.org (accessed May 10, 2010).

Chapter 3
The New and Improved "Highest Form of Patriotism"

1. The Media Research Center, "ABC Argues Voters Don't Really Want Contract with America," MediaWatch, February 1995, http://www.mrc.org/mediawatch/1995/watch19950201.asp (accessed April 22, 2010).

2. Real Clear Politics, "Pelosi: Town Hall Protesters Are 'Carrying Swastikas,'" video, August 5, 2009, http://www.realclearpolitics.com/video/2009/08/05/pelosi_town_hall_protesters_are_carrying_swastikas.html (accessed April 21, 2010).

3. Patricia Murphy, "Pelosi Calls Healthcare Protests 'Astroturf,'" *The Capitolist*, http://www.politicsdaily.com/2009/08/04/pelosi-calls-anger-over-health-care-reform-astroturf/ (accessed May 10, 2010).

4. RealClearPolitics.com, "Pelosi: Town Hall Protesters Are 'Carrying Swatiskas,'" http://www.realclearpolitics.com/video/2009/08/05/pelosi_town_hall_protesters_are_carrying_swastikas.html (accessed June 1, 2010).

5. Julia A. Seymour, "Media Cover Town Hall Outrage from Left, Calling It 'Orchestrated' and 'Not about Policy,'" Business and Media Institute, August 12, 2009, http://www.businessandmedia.org/articles/2009/20090812160547.aspx (accessed April 22, 2010).

6. Thomas L. Friedman, "Where Did 'We' Go?" *New York Times*, September 29, 2009, http://www.nytimes.com/2009/09/30/opinion/30friedman.html (accessed April 22, 2010).

7. Donny Deutsch, interview by Joy Behar, *The Joy Behar Show*, February 22, 2010, http://premium.asia.cnn.com/TRANSCRIPTS/1002/22/joy.01.html (accessed April 22, 2010).

8. Lachlan Markay, "Liberal Condescension Evident in Tea Party Coverage," NewBusters.org, February 8, 2010, http://newsbusters.org/blogs/lachlan-markay/2010/02/08/liberal-condescension-evident-tea-party-coverage (accessed May 10, 2010).

9. Noel Sheppard, "Maddow: Tea Party Conventioneers Are Racists in White Hoods," NewsBusters.org, February 6, 2010, http://newsbusters.org/blogs/noel-sheppard/2010/02/06/maddow-tea-party-conventioneers-are-racists-wearing-white-hoods (accessed May 10, 2010).

10. MilitaryConnection.com, "General David H. Petraeus Biography," http://www.militaryconnection.com/david-petraeus-bio.asp (accessed May 10, 2010).

11. General David Petraeus, interview by Hugh Hewitt, *The Hugh Hewitt Show*, transcript reported in Mike Hashimoto, "Iraq Report from the Front," *Dallas Morning News*, July 19, 2007, http://dallasmorningviewsblog.dallasnews.com/archives/2007/07/iraq-report-fro.html (accessed May 10, 2010).

12. "General Petraeus or General Betray Us?" *New York Times* ad pdf posted by MoveOn.org, September 10, 2007, http://pol.moveon.org/petraeus.html (accessed April 22, 2010).

13. Tim Dickinson, "Rolling Stone vs. MoveOn.org," Real Clear Politics, September 10, 2007, http://realclearpolitics.blogs.time.com/2007/09/10/rolling_stone_vs_move onorg/ (accessed April 29, 2010).

14. Peter D. Feaver, "MoveOn's McCarthy moment," *Boston Globe*, September 11, 2007, http://www.boston.com/news/globe/editorial_opinion/oped/articles/2007/09/11/moveons_mccarthy_moment/ (accessed April 22, 2010).

15. Michael Dobbs, "General Betray Us?" *Washington Post* Fact Checker, http://blog.washingtonpost.com/fact-checker/2007/09/general_betray_us.html (accessed April 22, 2010).

16. For example, Senator Barbara Boxer used up her entire question time allotment in making a speech in which she implied that General Petraeus was intellectually dishonest and that she was more informed about the situation on the ground in Iraq than he—leaving no time for General Petraeus to respond. Thomas B. Edsall, "Questioning Petraeus: Squandered Opportunities, Longwinded Monologues," *Huffington Post*, September 19, 2007, http://www.huffingtonpost.com/2007/09/19/questioning-petraeus-squ_n_65101.html?view=screen (accessed April 22, 2010).

CHAPTER 4
AMERICAN IDOLATRY

1. ScienceDaily.com, "Pop Stars More Than Twice as Likely to Die an Early Death," September 4, 2007, http://www.sciencedaily.com/releases/2007/09/070903204815.htm (accessed April 22, 2010).

2. *Sydney Morning Herald*, "Celebrity Worship Addictive: Study," August 14, 2003, http://www.smh.com.au/articles/2003/08/14/1060588497208.html (accessed April 22, 2010).

3. American Academy of Achievement, "Norman Borlaug Biography," http://www.achievement.org/autodoc/page/bor0bio-1 (accessed April 22, 2010).

4. The World Food Prize, "WFP Founder Norman Borlaug Receives America's Highest Civilian Honor," http://www.worldfoodprize.org/press_room/2006/december/borlaug-congressional.htm (accessed April 22, 2010).

5. Jonathan Alter, "He Only Saved a Billion People," *Newsweek*, http://www.newsweek.com/id/32864/page/1 (accessed April 22, 2010).

6. Kris Hollington, *Wolves, Jackals, and Foxes: The Assassins Who Changed History* (New York: St. Martin's Press, 2007), 154.

CHAPTER 5
STUCK IN THE '60S

1. The popular term was first used by the Union of Democratic Control in 1914 in their pacifist manifesto. It became a favorite boogeyman for antiwar protesters in the 1960s.

2. Greg Barber, "Days of Protest," *The Online NewsHour,* PBS.org, April 28, 2000, http://www.pbs.org/newshour/bb/asia/vietnam/protests.html (accessed April 22, 2010).

3. Jim Miklaszewski and Mike Viqueira, "Lawmaker: Marines Killed Iraqis 'in Cold Blood,'" MSNBC, May 17, 2006, http://www.msnbc.msn.com/id/12838343/ (accessed April 22, 2010).

4. Richard Gazarik, "Marine Files Defamation Suit Against Murtha," *TribLive,* August 3, 2006, http://www.pittsburghlive.com/x/pittsburghtrib/s_464567.html (accessed April 22, 2010).

5. *Weekly Standard,* "Hollywood Hates the Troops," August 31, 2007, http://www .weeklystandard.com/Content/Public/Articles/000/000/014/041llllv.asp (accessed April 22, 2010).

6. As of April 2010, a minimum figure of 95,934 deaths was put forward by the Iraq Body Count Web site, an antiwar Web site that claims to tally all civilian deaths in Iraq as reported in the news media. The aim of the count is to hold the United States and Britain accountable for a wide range of civilian deaths. As the site states: "The count encompasses noncombatants killed by military or paramilitary action and the breakdown in civil security following the invasion." Iraq Body Count, www .iraqbodycount.org.

7. Baghdad Diarist (Pvt. Scott Thomas Beauchamp), "Shock Troops," *New Republic,* July 13, 2007, http://www.tnr.com/article/shock-troops (accessed April 22, 2010).

8. Marcus Baram, "Pentagon: Baghdad Diarist Writes Fiction," ABC News, August 7, 2007, http://www.abcnews.go.com/US/story?id=3455826&page=1 (accessed April 22, 2010).

9. Bill Sammon, "Obama's Comments on Afghanistan Draw Sharp Rebuke from Romney Campaign," Examiner.com, August 14, 2007, http://www.examiner.com/a -880543~Obama_s_comments_on_Afghanistan_draw_sharp_rebuke_from_Romney _campaign.html (accessed April 22, 2010).

10. Geoffrey Dickens, "Chris Matthews Riffs with Anti-war Rockers Crosby and Nash," NewsBusters, October 15, 2007, http://newsbusters.org/blogs/geoffrey-dickens/ 2007/10/15/chris-matthews-riffs-anti-war-rockers-crosby-nash (accessed April 22, 2010).

11. Roderick Boyd, "A CNN Executive Says G.I.s in Iraq Target Journalists," *New York Sun,* February 8, 2005, http://www.nysun.com/article/8866 (accessed April 22, 2010).

12. Sharon Kehnemui Liss, "Durbin Apologizes for Nazi, Gulag, Pol Pot Remarks," FoxNews.com, June 22, 2005, http://www.foxnews.com/story/0,2933,160275,00.html (accessed April 22, 2010).

CHAPTER 6
BLAMING THE VICTIM: ISRAEL AS SCAPEGOAT

1. Benjamin Netanyahu, "Remarks as Delivered by Former Israeli Prime Minister," speech, AIPAC Conference, Washington DC, April 22, 2002, http://www.netanyahu.org/remasdelbyfo.html (accessed April 22, 2010).
2. Veronique Mistiaen, Jody K. Biel, and Elizabeth Bryant, "Fears of Anti-Semitism Sweep Europe/Leftists, Intellectuals Blaming Israel for World's Ills," *San Francisco Chronicle*, December 14, 2003, http://articles.sfgate.com/2003-12-14/news/17522285_1_semitism-jews-criticism-of-israeli-policies (accessed April 22, 2010).
3. Peter Beaumont, "Israel Outraged as EU Poll Names It a Threat to Peace," *The Observer*, November 2, 2003, http://www.guardian.co.uk/world/2003/nov/02/israel.eu (accessed May 12, 2010).
4. Mistiaen, Biel, and Bryant, "Fears of Anti-Semitism Sweep Europe/Leftists, Intellectuals Blaming Israel for World's Ills."
5. Eric Hoffer, "Israel's Peculiar Position," *Los Angeles Times*, May 26, 1968, sec. G7.
6. LATimes.com, "Arafat Missed Chance to Create Palestinian State," November 16, 2004, http://articles.latimes.com/2004/nov/16/opinion/le-peterson16.2 (accessed May 10, 2010).
7. Mark Steyn, "The Most Wrecked People on Earth," National Review Online, March 27, 2006, http://www.nationalreview.com/issue/steyn200603270647.asp (accessed April 22, 2010).

CHAPTER 7
PHONY OUTRAGE

1. Proverbs 26:27.
2. Zogby International, "President George W. Bush and U.S. Congress Register Record-Low Approval Ratings in New Reuters/Zogby Poll," http://www.zogby.com/NEWS/readnews.cfm?ID=1359 (accessed May 12, 2010).
3. Media Matters for America, "Limbaugh: Service Members Who Support U.S. Withdrawal Are 'Phony Soldiers,'" September 27, 2007, http://mediamatters.org/research/200709270010 (accessed May 12, 2010).
4. Byron York, "Limbaugh Makes His Case," National Review Online, October 3, 2007, http://article.nationalreview.com/329304/limbaugh-makes-his-case/byron-york (accessed May 12, 2010).
5. Ibid.
6. Harry Reid, "Reid Calls on Senators to Join in Condemning Limbaugh's Attack on Our Troops," statement on the floor of the U.S. Senate, October 1, 2007, Democrats.Senate.gov, http://democrats.senate.gov/newsroom/record.cfm?id=284592 (accessed April 23, 2010).
7. Amanda Terkel, "Harkin: 'Maybe Limbaugh Was High on Drugs Again,'" Think Progress, October 1, 2007, http://thinkprogress.org/2007/10/01/harkin-maybe-limbaugh-was-high-on-drugs-again/ (accessed April 23, 2010).
8. York, "Limbaugh Makes His Case."
9. Ibid.

10. Ibid.

11. Ibid.; Associated Press, "Phony Soldier Charged With Making Up Claims of Atrocities in Iraq," FOXNews.com, May 20, 2007, http://www.foxnews.com/story/0,2933,274097,00.html (accessed May 12, 2010).

12. John Kerry, testimony before the Senate Foreign Relations Committee, Washington DC, April 22, 1971, https://facultystaff.richmond.edu/~ebolt/history398/johnkerrytestimony.html (accessed April 23, 2010).

13. Reid, "Reid Calls on Senators."

14. Ibid.

15. Politico, "Clear Channel CEO Responds to Reid," October 2, 2007, http://www.politico.com/static/PPM43_071002_reidletter.html (accessed May 12, 2010).

16. FOXNews.com, "Limbaugh Letter Fetches $2.1 Million on eBay," October 21, 2007, http://www.foxnews.com/story/0,2933,303569,00.html (accessed April 23, 2010).

17. Ibid.

18. *Rush Limbaugh Show*, "Limbaugh: I Hope Obama Fails," transcript of radio program, January 16, 2009, http://www.rushlimbaugh.com/home/daily/site_011609/content/01125113.guest.html (accessed April 23, 2010).

CHAPTER 8
DEFINING DICTATORSHIP DOWN

1. CNN.com, *Showbiz Tonight*, March 24, 2006, transcript, http://transcripts.cnn.com/TRANSCRIPTS/0603/24/sbt.01.html (accessed April 23, 2010).

2. Len Hart, "How George Bush Became a Dictator," The Existentialist Cowboy, July 25, 2006, http://existentialistcowboy.blogspot.com/2006/07/how-george-bush-became-dictator.html (accessed April 23, 2010).

3. Kaye Ross, "Nader Calls Bush 'Dictator,'" *San Jose Mercury News*, March 23, 2003, http://www.commondreams.org/headlines03/0323-09.htm (accessed April 23, 2010).

4. Associated Press, "Belafonte: Bush 'Greatest Terrorist in the World,'" MSNBC.com, January 8, 2006, http://www.msnbc.msn.com/id/10767465/ (accessed April 23, 2010).

5. CNN.com, "Interview With Sean Penn," *Larry King Live*, September 14, 2006, http://transcripts.cnn.com/TRANSCRIPTS/0609/14/lkl.01.html (accessed April 23, 2010).

6. Jonathan Alter, "Bush's Snoopgate," *Newsweek*, December 19, 2005, http://www.newsweek.com/id/51320 (accessed April 23, 2010).

7. Jack Cafferty, "Many Lawmakers Outraged at Phone Record Tracking...," *The Situation Room*, May 11, 2006, http://transcripts.cnn.com/TRANSCRIPTS/0605/11/sitroom.01.html (accessed April 23, 2010).

8. Rachel Aspden, "Special Issue: The World's Top 10 Dictators," *New Statesman*, September 4, 2006, http://www.newstatesman.com/200609040067 (accessed April 23, 2010).

9. Andrew Meldrum, "Zimbabwe Inflation 'to Hit 1.5M%,'" Guardian.co.uk, June 21, 2007, http://www.guardian.co.uk/world/2007/jun/21/zimbabwe.andrewmeldrum (accessed May 13, 2010).

Chapter 9
Palin Derangement Syndrome

1. Cinnamon Stillwell, "Palin Derangement Syndrome: Obama's Worst Enemy?" *San Francisco Chronicle,* September 18, 2008, http://articles.sfgate.com/2008-09-18/opinion/17120134_1_palin-s-selection-hillary-clinton-voters-national-review (accessed May 13, 2010).

2. "Sarah Palin's Palm Cheat-sheet Steals Her Show," *Washington Post,* http://voices.washingtonpost.com/44/2010/02/sarah-palins-palm-cheat-sheet.html (accessed April 23, 2010).

3. Noel Sheppard, "Matthews Attacks Palin for 12 Minutes: 'Can a Palm Reader be President?' 'Is She a Balloon Head?'" NewsBusters, February 9, 2010, http://newsbusters.org/blogs/noel-sheppard/2010/02/08/matthews-attacks-sarah-palm-reader-palin-she-balloon-head (accessed April 23, 2010).

4. Brad Wilmouth, "FNC: Feinstein Cheated in Debate Using Palin-Like Hand Notes," NewsBusters.org, February 24, 2010, http://newsbusters.org/blogs/brad-wilmouth/2010/02/24/fnc-feinstein-cheated-debate-using-palin-hand-notes (accessed May 13, 2010).

Chapter 10
Summary (Part 1)

1. Pamela Jean, "The Boy Scouts of America Ban Gays—Philadelphia Raises Their Rent by $199,999," DigitalJournal.com, October 19, 2007, http://www.digitaljournal.com/article/241379 (accessed May 13, 2010).

2. Heather MacDonald, "Why the Boy Scouts Work," *City Journal,* Winter 2000, http://www.city-journal.org/html/10_1_why_the_boy.html (accessed April 23, 2010).

3. Dennis Prager, "Judeo-Christian Values, Part 11: Moral Absolutes," World Net Daily, May 3, 2005, http://www.worldnetdaily.com/news/article.asp?ARTICLE_ID=44093 (accessed April 23, 2010).

4. Romans 1:25.

5. John 14:6, emphasis added.

6. John 18:37, NIV.

7. John 18:38, NIV.

Part 2 Overview

1. Life in a Jar: The Irena Sendler Project, http://www.irenasendler.org/ (accessed May 9, 2010).

2. Angela Carter, *Wise Children* (New York: Farrar, Straus and Giroux, 1991), 115, http://books.google.com/books?id=x9WbNMVXAj8C&printsec=frontcover&dq=wise+children+angela+carter&cd=1#v=onepage&q=life%20and%20death&f=false (accessed April 23, 2010).

3. Colin Nickerson, "Traveling Cadaver Show Wants You: Body Exhibit Seeks Donors in Boston," *Boston Globe,* July 9, 2006, http://www.boston.com/news/world/

europe/articles/2006/07/09/traveling_cadaver_show_wants_you/ (accessed April 23, 2010).

4. Ibid.

5. Holland Cotter, "Butchered Body Parts and Ideas of Childhood," *New York Times*, September 1, 1995, sec. Arts.

6. For example, the Norwegian black metal group Dimmu Borgir saw their album *In Sorte Diaboli* (Latin for "in direct contact with Satan") debut at #43 on the Billboard Top 200 album charts the week of May 12, 2007. "In Sorte Diaboli," Billboard.com, http://www.billboard.com/#/album/dimmu-borgir/in-sorte-diaboli/906198 (accessed May 14, 2010).

7. Wikipedia.com, s.v. "Death Metal," http://en.wikipedia.org/wiki/Death_metal (accessed April 23, 2010).

8. Ibid.

CHAPTER 11
VIRTUOUS ABORTION

1. "Secretary of State Hillary Clinton's Remarks at National Prayer Breakfast," February 4, 2010, http://secretaryclinton.wordpress.com/2010/02/04/secretary-of-state-hillary-clintons-remarks-at-the-national-prayer-breakfast/ (accessed May 9, 2010).

2. Steven Ertelt, "Blythe Danner, Gwyneth Paltrow Exploit Mother's Day for Abortion Fundraising," LifeNews.com, May 10, 2006, http://www.lifenews.com/nat2254.html (accessed April 23, 2010).

3. Ibid.

4. For information about study done in England about regrets of abortion, see Steven Ertelt, "British Survey Finds Overwhelming Majority of Women Regretted Abortions," LifeNews.com, September 12, 2006, http://www.lifenews.com/nat2579.html (accessed May 14, 2010).

5. NPR.org, "NPR Changes Abortion Language," March 24, 2010, http://www.npr.org/ombudsman/2010/03/npr_changes_abortion_language.html (accessed May 14, 2010). Also see, Lachlan Markay, "NPR Ditches 'Pro-Life' Label for 'Abortion Rights Opponent' Tag in News Reports," LifeNews.com, March 25, 2010, http://www.lifenews.com/nat6195.html (accessed May 14, 2010).

6. *Ms.*, "'We Had Abortions': Ms. Magazine Expands Campaign for Honesty and Freedom," (press release, October 4, 2006), http://www.msmagazine.com/press/2006-mspetition.asp (accessed April 23, 2010).

7. *Ms.*, "Ms. Delivers 'We Had Abortions' Signatures to White House and Congress," (press release, January 22, 2007), http://www.msmagazine.com/press/2007-mspetition.asp (accessed April 23, 2010).

8. WorldNetDaily.com, "Lawmakers Vote to 'Celebrate' Abortion," January 24, 2004, http://www.worldnetdaily.com/news/article.asp?ARTICLE_ID=36757 (accessed April 23, 2010).

9. Girl-Mom.com, http://www.girl-mom.com (accessed April 23, 2010).

10. Kaya, "I Chose Abortion and I Am Proud by Kaya," Girl-Mom.com, http://www.girl-mom.com/node/139 (accessed May 14, 2010).

CHAPTER 12
"MR. SMITH, YOUR ORDER OF STEM CELLS IS READY"

1. Brendan Nyhan, "The Phony Attack on Bush's Stem Cell Research 'Ban,'" Spinsanity.org, August 17, 2004, http://www.spinsanity.org/post.html?2004_08_15_archive.html (accessed April 23, 2010).

2. Ramesh Ponnuru, *The Party of Death: The Democrats, the Media, the Courts, and the Disregard for Human Life* (Washington DC: Regnery Publishing, 2006), 144.

3. Kathryn Jean Lopez, "Doc Hollywood on the Campaign Trail," National Review Online, October 24, 2006, http://article.nationalreview.com/?q=MzcwMGRkMjg2M WVhZWIxYTY0N2NmNTYwNDMzMGQ2M2Q= (accessed April 23, 2010).

4. Writing of California's five-year, multibillion dollar, taxpayer-financed research program in embryonic stem cell research, Joe Carter wrote in the journal *First Things*: "The battle over embryonic stem cell research is over. A few skirmishes will no doubt continue—perhaps even for years—and some ESCR advocates will refuse to acknowledge defeat. But they have decisively lost. Years from now, when we look back in astonishment at having been fleeced for billions to pay for therapeutically worthless research, we'll recognize that California was the Waterloo for ESCR....But five years [after California's Proposition 71], the hype has died down and ESCR has provided no cures, no therapies, no progress, and no hope." Joe Carter, "The Waterloo for Embryonic Stem Cell Research," *First Things*, January 13, 2010, http://www.firstthings.com/blogs/firstthoughts/2010/01/13/the-waterloo-for-embryonic-stem-cell-research/ (accessed April 23, 2010).

5. Rob Stein, "Researchers May Have Found Equivalent of Embryonic Stem Cells," *Washington Post*, July 24, 2009, http://www.washingtonpost.com/wp-dyn/content/article/2009/07/23/AR2009072301786.html (accessed April 23, 2010); see also, Do No Harm, http://www.stemcellresearch.org/.

6. Matthew Hill, "Ukraine Babies in Stem Cell Probe," BBC News, http://news.bbc.co.uk/2/hi/europe/6171083.stm (accessed May 14, 2010).

CHAPTER 13
IF THIS IS YOUR MERCY, I'D HATE TO SEE YOUR VENGEANCE

1. CNN.com, "Anderson Cooper 360 Degrees," April 16, 2010, http://transcripts.cnn.com/TRANSCRIPTS/1004/16/acd.02.html (accessed May 9, 2010).

2. Ponnuru, *The Party of Death*, 121.

3. American Medical Association, "Opinion 2.211—Physician-Assisted Suicide," http://www.ama-assn.org/ama/pub/physician-resources/medical-ethics/code-medical-ethics/opinion2211.shtml (accessed April 24, 2010).

4. Leon R. Kass, "I Will Give No Deadly Drug: Why Doctors Must Not Kill," American College of Surgeons, http://www.facs.org/education/ethics/kasslect.html (accessed April 24, 2010), quoting from Y. Kamisar, "Some Nonreligious Views Against Proposed 'Mercy Killing' Legislation," *Minnesota Law Review* 42 (1958): 969–1042, [Reprinted, with a new preface by Kamisar, in "The Slide Toward Mercy Killing," *Child and Family Reprint Booklet Series*, 1987].

5. "Rescue the Perishing" by Fanny J. Crosby. Public domain.

6. Charles Krauthammer, "First and Last, Do No Harm," *TIME*, April 15, 1996, http://www.time.com/time/magazine/article/0,9171,984390,00.html (accessed April 24, 2010).

7. Ibid.

8. Family Research Council newsletter, August 1998.

9. Angie Drobnic Holan, "PolitiFact's Lie of the Year: 'Death Panels,'" *St. Petersburg Times,* PolitiFact.com, December 18, 2009, http://www.politifact.com/truth-o-meter/article/2009/dec/18/politifact-lie-year-death-panels/ (accessed April 24, 2010).

10. Alan Reynolds, "Death Panels? Sarah Palin Was Right," Cato @ Liberty, http://www.cato-at-liberty.org/2009/12/22/death-panels-sarah-palin-was-right/ (accessed April 24, 2010).

11. George Stephanopoulos, "Gingrich Defends Palin's 'Death Panels,'" *George's Bottom Line*, ABC News, August 9, 2009, http://blogs.abcnews.com/george/2009/08/gingrich-defends-palins-death-panels-.html (accessed April 24, 2010).

12. Bob Unruh, "N.Y. Times Columnist: Death Panels Will Save 'a Lot of Money,'" WorldNetDaily.com, March 30, 2010, http://www.wnd.com/index.php?pageId=134401 (accessed May 9, 2010).

Chapter 14
Trample the Poor, Pretend to Save the Earth

1. Paul Driessen, "May You Freeze in the Dark," Townhall.com, December 22, 2007, http://www.townhall.com/columnists/PaulDriessen/2007/12/22/may_you_freeze_in_the_dark?page=full&comments=true (accessed April 24, 2010).

2. Ibid.

3. Ibid.

4. Ibid.

5. Ibid.

6. Ibid.

7. Ibid.

8. Luke 3:11.

9. Richard and Rhoda Goldman Fund, "2007 Grants," http://www.goldmanfund.org/html/grants/awarded/2007/2007-grants-population.html (accessed April 24, 2010).

10. The Goldman Fund distributed more than $6.2 million in "population grants" in 2007 alone. Ibid.

11. Driessen, "May You Freeze in the Dark."

Chapter 15
Silent Summer

1. Tina Rosenberg, "What the World Needs Now Is DDT," *New York Times*, April 11, 2004, http://www.nytimes.com/2004/04/11/magazine/what-the-world-needs-now-is-ddt.html?sec=health?pagewanted=1 (accessed April 25, 2010).

2. Richard Carter and Kamini N. Mendis, "Evolutionary and Historical Aspects of the Burden of Malaria," PubMed Central, American Society for Microbiology,

October 15, 2002, http://www.pubmedcentral.nih.gov/articlerender.fcgi?tool
=pubmed&pubmedid=12364370

3. Rosenberg, "What the World Needs Now Is DDT."

4. Marjorie Mazel Hecht, "Bring Back DDT, and Science With It!" *21st Century
Science & Technology Magazine*, Summer 2002, http://www.21stcenturysciencetech
.com/articles/summ02/DDT.html#The%20Silent%20Spring%20Fraud (accessed April
25, 2010).

5. J. Gordon Edwards, "The Lies of Rachel Carson," *21st Century Science &
Technology Magazine* (Summer 1992), http://www.21stcenturysciencetech.com/
articles/summ02/Carson.html (accessed April 25, 2010).

6. Jay H. Lehr, ed., *Standard Handbook of Environmental Science, Health, and
Technology* (New York: McGraw-Hill, 2000), 6.24.

7. JunkScience.com, "The Malaria Clock: A Green Eco-Imperialist Legacy of
Death," http://junkscience.com/malaria_clock.html (accessed April 25, 2010).

8. FixHealthCarePolicy.com, "Video of the Week: 'We Have to Pass the Bill So You
Can Find Out What Is in It," March 10, 2010, http://fixhealthcarepolicy.com/in-the
-news/video-of-the-week-we-have-to-pass-the-bill-so-you-can-find-out-what-is-in-it/
(accessed May 15, 2010).

9. National Public Radio, "Malaria," April 18, 1997, http://www.npr.org/templates/
story/story.php?storyId=1010611 (accessed May 15, 2010).

10. Rosenberg, "What the World Needs Now Is DDT."

11. Ibid.

12. JunkScience.com, "The Malaria Clock."

CHAPTER 16
THE GLOBAL WAR AGAINST BABY GIRLS

1. National Organization for Women, "NOW Calls on Senate to Reject Ashcroft
for Attorney General," press release, January 31, 2001, posted by Common Dreams
Progressive Newswire, http://www.commondreams.org/news2001/0131-01.htm
(accessed April 25, 2010).

2. Patricia Ireland, "NOW Opposes Ashcroft and Thompson," press release,
January 16, 2001, National Organization for Women, http://www.now.org/press/01
-01/1-16-00.html (accessed April 25, 2010).

3. Morgaine, "Stop Alito—Save American Democracy," What She Said! January 8,
2006, http://the-goddess.org/whatshesaid/2006/01/stop-alito-save-american-democracy
.html (accessed May 15, 2010).

4. National Organization for Women, "Newsflash: Restrictions on Legal Abortions
Increasing. Women Refused Access to Birth Control. Access to Justice Denied,"
http://www.now.org/issues/judicial/supreme/defeatalito.html (accessed April 25, 2010).

5. Katherine Kersten, "Why Are American Feminists Silent on the Plight of Muslim
Women?" *Minneapolis Star-Tribune*, May 22, 2007, http://kerstenblog.startribune.com/
kerstenblog/?cat=83 (accessed April 25, 2010).

6. "DHAKA, Bangladesh—Alarmed by a growing spate of acid attacks targeting
young women, the Bangladeshi government has proposed introducing a maximum
penalty of death for offenders. A recent survey has shown that almost 250 people,

mostly women, were severely burnt in corrosive acid attacks last year compared with 200 the previous year." CNN.com, "Bangladesh Acid Attackers May Face Death," February 5, 2002, http://archives.cnn.com/2002/WORLD/asiapcf/south/02/05/bangladesh.acid/ (accessed April 25, 2010).

7. The woman was later pardoned by the king of Saudi Arabia in response to pressure from the U.S. government. CBSNews.com, "Saudi King Pardons Rape Victim," December 17, 2007, http://www.cbsnews.com/stories/2007/12/17/world/main3624734.shtml?source=RSSattr=World_3624734 (accessed April 25, 2010).

8. Harvey Mansfield, "At Universities, Little Learned from 9/11," *Boston Globe*, September 13, 2006, http://www.boston.com/news/globe/editorial_opinion/oped/articles/2006/09/13/at_universities_little_learned_from_911/ (accessed April 25, 2010).

9. Equality Now, "Equality Now Adolescent Girls' Legal Defense Fund," http://www.equalitynow.org/english/index.html (accessed April 25, 2010).

10. Benazir Bhutto, "Islam Forbids Injustice Against People, Nations and Women," address to the Fourth World Conference on Women, Beijing, September 4, 1995, http://www.ppp.org.pk/mbb/speeches/speeche49.html (accessed April 25, 2010).

11. Ibid.

12. Amelia Gentleman, "India's Lost Daughters: Abortion Toll in Millions," *New York Times*, January 9, 2006, http://www.nytimes.com/2006/01/09/world/asia/09iht-india.html (accessed April 25, 2010).

13. Gudrun Schultz, "7,000 Unborn Girls Die from Sex-Selection Abortion Daily in India," LifeSiteNews.com, December 14, 2006, http://www.lifesitenews.com/ldn/2006/dec/06121401.html (accessed April 25, 2010).

14. Gentleman, "India's Lost Daughters."

15. Gudrun, "7,000 Unborn Girls Die."

16. Ibid.

17. Ibid.

18. Ken Blackwell, "Protecting the Human Dignity of the Girl Child Worldwide," Townhall.com. November 1, 2007, http://www.townhall.com/columnists/KenBlackwell/2007/11/01/protecting_the_human_dignity_of_the_girl_child_worldwide (accessed April 25, 2010).

CHAPTER 17
WHAT GENOCIDE?

1. Elise Labott, "Google Earth Maps Out Darfur Atrocities," CNN.com, April 15, 2007, http://www.cnn.com/2007/TECH/04/10/google.genocide/ (accessed May 15, 2010).

2. Joan B. King Institute for Peace and Justice, "Peace and Justice Update, vol. 15, no. 4," March 9, 2007, page 7, http://www.sandiego.edu/peacestudies/documents/ipj/reports/PJUpdates/Sp07UpdatesPDF/UpdateVolume15Number04.pdf (accessed May 15, 2010).

3. Paul H. Liben, "Murder in the Sudan," *First Things*, August/September 1995, http://www.firstthings.com/article.php3?id_article=4078 (accessed April 26, 2010).

4. Ibid.

5. Nat Hentoff wrote: "For several years, the new American abolitionist movement has been trying to get Jesse Jackson to at least publicly condemn slavery in

Sudan. Madison and others felt that since Jackson was a key force in focusing public consciousness on apartheid in South Africa, he would be of great help in combating the enslavement and gang rapes in Sudan that I've been writing about in this column." Nat Hentoff, "Who Will Succeed Jesse Jackson?" *Village Voice*, March 6, 2001, http://radio.villagevoice.com/news/0110,hentoff,22797,6.html (accessed April 26, 2010).

6. Anti-Defamation League, "Farrakhan and the Nation of Islam on Slavery in Sudan," http://www.adl.org/issue_nation_of_islam/farrakhan_and_slavery_in_sudan.asp (accessed April 26, 2010).

7. William Reed, "Take Another Look at the 'Save Darfur' Crowd," FinalCall.com, updated January 4, 2008, http://www.finalcall.com/artman/publish/article_4231.shtml (accessed April 26, 2010).

CHAPTER 18
STERILIZED FOR THE PLANET

1. Rod Parsley, *Culturally Incorrect: How Clashing Worldviews Affect Your Future* (Nashville: Thomas Nelson, 2007), 40.

2. David M. Graber, "Mother Nature as a Hothouse Flower," *Los Angeles Times* Book Review, October 22, 1989, quoted in Glenn Woiceshyn, "Environmentalism and Eco-Terrorism," *Capitalism Magazine*, September 30, 1998, http://www.capitalismmagazine.com/index.php?news=197 (accessed May 15, 2010).

3. As quoted in Deroy Murdock, "Some Greens Love Earth Best When It's Shoveled Over Fellow Humans," *Free Lance-Star*, July 7, 2006, http://news.google.com/newspapers?nid=1298&dat=20060707&id=wC4zAAAAIBAJ&sjid=fAgGAAAAIBAJ&pg=4074,1775528 (accessed May 15, 2010).

4. Jay Richards, "There Are More Environmentalist Misanthropes Than You Think," Acton Institute PowerBlog, June 12, 2006, http://blog.acton.org/archives/962-there-are-more-environmentalist-misanthropes-than-you-think.html (accessed April 26, 2010).

5. Natasha Courtenay-Smith and Morag Turner, "Meet the Women Who Won't Have Babies—Because They're Not Eco Friendly," *Daily Mail*, November 21, 2007, http://www.dailymail.co.uk/pages/live/femail/article.html?in_article_id=495495&in_page_id=1879 (accessed April 26, 2010).

6. Ibid.

7. Ibid.

8. Mark Steyn, "It's the Demography, Stupid," *New Criterion*, as viewed in *Wall Street Journal*, January 4, 2006, http://opinionjournal.com/extra/?id=110007760 (accessed May 15, 2010).

9. Genesis 2:15; 1:28.

10. As quoted in "The Pro-Americanism of a French Intellectual," *Baltimore Reporter*, April 27, 2008, http://www.baltimorereporter.com/?p=5317 (accessed May 15, 2010).

CHAPTER 19
SUMMARY (PART 2)

1. Deuteronomy 30:19.

2. John 14:6, NKJV.

3. John 10:10, NKJV.

4. 1 Corinthians 15:55, NKJV.

5. Peggy Noonan, "The Culture of Death," OrthodoxyToday.org, (originally published in *Wall Street Journal*, April 22, 1999), http://www.orthodoxytoday.org/articles2/NoonanCulture.shtml (accessed April 26, 2010).

6. Ibid.

Part 3 Overview

1. Kate Santich, "The Age of Innocence Quickly Fades," AccessMyLibrary.com (originally published in the *Orlando Sentinel*, April 22, 2007), http://www.accessmylibrary.com/coms2/summary_0286-30370431_ITM (accessed April 26, 2010).

2. WSBTV.com, "Three Young Boys Arrested in Rape Case," November 19, 2007, http://www.wsbtv.com/news/14635513/detail.html (accessed April 26, 2010).

Chapter 20
Men Will Be Boys

1. Ray Jackson, *America's Youngest Warriors: Stories About the Young Men and Women Who Served in the Armed Forces of the United States of America Before Attaining Legal Age* (n.p.: Veterans of Underage Military Service, 1996).

2. *Good Morning America*, "Young Warriors: Some Veterans Lied About Their Ages," ABCNews.com, November 11, 2007, http://abcnews.go.com/GMA/story?id=3850523&page=1 (accessed April 26, 2010).

3. Ibid.

4. James Lileks, "The Bleat: March 7, 2002," Lileks.com, http://www.lileks.com/bleats/archive/02/0302/030102.html (accessed April 26, 2010).

5. 1 Corinthians 13:11, NKJV.

6. Diana West, *The Death of the Grown-Up: How America's Arrested Development Is Bringing Down Western Civilization* (New York: St. Martin's Press, 2007), 1.

7. U.S. Census Bureau, "Families and Living Arrangements," http://www.census.gov/population/www/socdemo/hh-fam.html (accessed May 15, 2010).

8. Mike Males, "Enabling Adult Immaturity," *Youth Today*, http://www.youthtoday.org/publication/article.cfm?article_id=747 (accessed May 15, 2010).

Chapter 21
Big Mother Is Listening

1. Ezra Levant, "What a Strange Place Canada Is," *Globe and Mail*, January 21, 2008, http://www.theglobeandmail.com/servlet/story/RTGAM.20080120.wcomment0121/BNStory/National/home (accessed April 26, 2010).

2. Ibid.

3. Marni Soupcoff, "Ezra Levant: Censorship in the Name of 'Human Rights,'" *National Post*, December 17, 2007, http://network.nationalpost.com/np/blogs/

fullcomment/archive/2007/12/17/ezra-levant-censorship-in-the-name-of-human-rights
.aspx (accessed April 26, 2010).

4. Mark Steyn, "Alien Ideologies," National Review Online, January 6, 2008, http://corner.nationalreview.com/post/?q=NjY1YWJhNDc5ZTkyYzE4NTE3NTY yM2Q1ZTBkZjIxYzQ= (accessed April 26, 2010).

5. Ibid.

6. Ezra Levant, "Censorship in the Name of 'Human Rights,'" NationalPost.com, December 18, 2007, http://www.nationalpost.com/opinion/story.html?id=175234&p=1 (accessed May 15, 2010).

7. CBC News.com, "Court Quashes Human Rights Anti-gay Ruling," December 4, 2009, http://www.cbc.ca/canada/calgary/story/2009/12/04/calgary-court-gay-human -rights-ruling.html (accessed April 26, 2010).

Chapter 22
Pretty Babies

1. Stacy Weiner, "Goodbye to Girlhood," *Washington Post*, February 20, 2007, http://www.washingtonpost.com/wp-dyn/content/article/2007/02/16/ AR2007021602263.html (accessed April 26, 2010).

2. American Psychological Association, "Report of the APA Task Force on the Sexualization of Girls" (2007), http://www.apa.org/pi/women/programs/girls/report .aspx (accessed April 26, 2010).

3. Jill Parkin, "Trash the Plastic Slappers," *Courier-Mail*, March 20, 2007, http:// www.couriermail.com.au/lifestyle/trash-the-plastic-slappers/story-e6frer4f -1111113190710 (accessed April 26, 2010).

4. Randy Hicks, "Marketing What? To Whom?" *Houston Chronicle*, March 21, 2007.

5. Vikki Ortiz, "Parents Say Kid's Thong Is Just Plain Wrong," *Milwaukee Journal Sentinal*, JS Online, May 17, 2002 http://www3.jsonline.com/story/index.aspx?id=43941 (accessed April 26, 2010).

6. Ibid.

7. Ibid.

8. Colin Fernandez, "Tesco Condemned for Selling Pole Dancing Toy," *Daily Mail*, October 24, 2006, http://www.dailymail.co.uk/pages/live/articles/news/news.html?in_ article_id=412195&in_page_id=17 (accessed April 26, 2010).

9. Ibid.

Chapter 23
Librarians for Defilement

1. American Library Association, "Book on Text Messaging Teens Prompts Most Book Challenges of 2009," press release, April 14, 2010, http://www.ala.org/ala/ newspresscenter/news/pressreleases2010/april2010/mostchallenged2009_oif.cfm (accessed April 26, 2010).

2. American Library Association, "Treasure Your Freedom to Read, Get Hooked on a Banned Book," press release, September 19, 2007, http://www.ala.org/ala/

newspresscenter/news/pressreleases2007/september2007/bbw07.cfm (accessed April 26, 2010).

3. The ALA's news release regarding "The Most Frequently Challenged Books of 2006" contained this paragraph: "Off the list this year, but on for several years past, are the *Catcher in the Rye* by J. D. Salinger, *Of Mice and Men* by John Steinbeck, and *The Adventures of Huckleberry Finn* by Mark Twain." American Library Association, "'And Tango Makes Three' Tops ALA's 2006 List of Most Challenged Books," press release, March 6, 2007, http://www.ala.org/ala/newspresscenter/news/pressreleases2007/march2007/mc06.cfm (accessed April 26, 2010).

4. American Library Association, "About Banned and Challenged Books," http://www.ala.org/ala/issuesadvocacy/banned/aboutbannedbooks/index.cfm (accessed May 15, 2010).

5. American Library Association, "Alaska Bill Would Give Parents Access to Children's Library Records," http://www.ala.org/ala/alonline/currentnews/newsarchive/alnews2004/february2004/alaskabill.cfm (accessed April 26, 2010).

6. American Library Association, "Intellectual Freedom and Censorship Q & A," http://www.ala.org/ala/aboutala/offices/oif/basics/ifcensorshipqanda.cfm (accessed April 26, 2010).

7. Janet M. LaRue, "Preventing Kids from Seeing Illegal Smut Is Not Unconstitutional; It's Common Sense," as quoted in SafeLibraries.org, "ALA's Double Standard on Censorship," http://www.safelibraries.org/ala-oif-doublestandard.htm (accessed May 15, 2010).

8. Walter Skold, "Librarians to Sever Ties with Scouts?" WorldNetDaily.com, April 22, 2006, http://www.worldnetdaily.com/news/article.asp?ARTICLE_ID=49860 (accessed April 26, 2010).

9. Art Moore, "Librarians Ignore Plea of Cuban Prisoners," WorldNetDaily.com, January 15, 2004, http://www.wnd.com/news/article.asp?ARTICLE_ID=36609 (accessed April 26, 2010).

10. Scott Savage, "Persecuted Librarian Censored Again," WorldNetDaily.com, May 9, 2006, http://www.worldnetdaily.com/news/article.asp?ARTICLE_ID=50115 (accessed April 26, 2010).

CHAPTER 24
MAKE ROOM FOR NANNY

1. Orwell, *1984*, 277.

2. George W. Bush, "Remarks on Labor Day in Richfield, Ohio," address, September 1, 2003, The American Presidency Project, http://www.presidency.ucsb.edu/ws/index.php?pid=63752&st=&st1= (accessed April 27, 2010).

3. Jacob Sullum, "Are You *Sure* You Want Fries with That?" Reason.com., October 26, 2007, http://www.reason.com/blog/show/123203.html (accessed April 27, 2010).

4. American Chesterton Society, "Quotations of G.K. Chesterton," http://www.chesterton.org/acs/quotes.htm (accessed April 27, 2010).

5. Nick Gillespie, "The Race to Ban What's Bad For Us," Reason.com, December 11, 2006, http://www.reason.com/news/show/117171.html (accessed April 27, 2010).

CHAPTER 25: IT TAKES ~~A VILLAGE~~ TWO PARENTS

1. Hillary Rodham Clinton, "Address to General Conference," address to General Conference of the United Methodist Church, Oklahoma City, April 24, 1996, http://gbgm-umc.org/mission/news/hillary.html (accessed April 27, 2010).

2. Nancy Pelosi, interview by Bob Schieffer, *Face the Nation*, January 7, 2007, http://www.cbsnews.com/htdocs/pdf/F1-7-7.pdf (accessed April 27, 2010).

3. Jonah Goldberg, "Child's Play," National Review Online, January 24, 2007, http://article.nationalreview.com/?q=MGFjNzBlYjc5NzJjNTg0ZGM0MzhkMmYxYW FlOWI3M2I= (accessed April 27, 2010).

4. Ibid.

5. Marian Wright Edelman, "An Open Letter to President Clinton From Marian Wright Edelman," November 3, 1995, http://econ161.berkeley.edu/politics/edelman_open_letter.html (accessed April 27, 2010).

6. Kay S. Hymowitz, "How Welfare Reform Worked," *City Journal*, Spring 2006, http://www.city-journal.org/html/16_2_welfare_reform.html (accessed April 27, 2010).

7. Mike Viquiera, "SChip Battle Heats Up," MSNBC First Read, October 18, 2007, http://firstread.msnbc.msn.com/archive/2007/10/18/417935.aspx (accessed April 27, 2010).

8. Luke 6:45, NKJV.

9. Sharon Jayson, "2-Parent Families Are Best, Study Shows," *USA Today*, September 13, 2005, reported in *Deseret News*, http://www.deseretnews.com/article/1,5143,6051541 63,00.html (accessed May 16, 2010).

10. Patrick Fagan and Robert Rector, "The Effects of Divorce on America," The Heritage Foundation, June 5, 2000, http://www.heritage.org/Research/Reports/2000/06/The-Effects-of-Divorce-on-America (accessed May 16, 2010).

11. Mark Steyn, "Stark Raving Madmen," National Review Online, October 21, 2007, http://article.nationalreview.com/331222/stark-raving-madmen/mark-steyn (accessed May 16, 2010).

12. Teddy Davis and Eloise Harper, "Clinton Floats $5,000 Baby Bond," ABC News, September 28, 2007, http://abcnews.go.com/Politics/story?id=3668781&page=1 (accessed April 27, 2010).

CHAPTER 26
ACADEMIC ADOLESCENCE

1. Betsy Morris, "Protests End Horowitz's Speech Early at Emory," *Columbia Spectator*, October 26, 2007, http://www.columbiaspectator.com/2007/10/26/protests -end-horowitz-s-speech-early-emory (accessed May 16, 2010).

2. Robert Spencer, "Emory U's President Apologizes to Horowitz," FrontPageMag .com, http://www.frontpagemag.com/Articles/Read.aspx?GUID=2E79EC67-75BA -4758-932D-9564B73FBDC4 (accessed April 27, 2010).

3. Rich Lowry, "McCain Delivers," National Review Online, May 19, 2006, http://corner.nationalreview.com/post/?q=N2EzYTBhMzUzZTU4ZWIwODM3NDM yN2FlOWE5ZmRiZ GI= (accessed April 27, 2010).

4. *Today*, "'Don't Tase Me, Bro' Student Breaks Silence," October 31, 2007, http://today.msnbc.msn.com/id/21558022/ns/today-today_people// (accessed April 27, 2010).

5. Ann Coulter, "Tase Him Bro!" AnnCoulter.com, September 26, 2007, http://www.anncoulter.com/cgi-local/printer_friendly.cgi?article=209 (accessed April 27, 2010).

6. George Leef, "Brandeis Administrators Go Bananas," Phi Beta Cons, National Review Online, January 24, 2008, http://phibetacons.nationalreview.com/post/?q=NGE4MGQwZmJlM2UzZWEzNmE1N2VjYjM0MmNlMzg4ZDY= (accessed April 27, 2010).

7. David Limbaugh, *Persecution: How Liberals Are Waging War Against Christianity* (New York: Regnery, 2003), 114.

8. Ibid.

9. John Leo, "PC: Almost Dead, Still Funny," *U.S. News and World Report*, November 27, 1994, http://www.usnews.com/usnews/opinion/articles/941205/archive_013763_2.htm (accessed May 16, 2010).

10. Susan McClary, *Feminine Endings: Music, Gender, and Sexuality* (Minneapolis: University of Minnesota Press, 2002), 7.

11. Ibid.

12. Ibid., 17.

13. Ibid., 18.

14. Mary Hiles, "Propagandizing Professors," FrontPageMag.com, January 23, 2008, http://www.frontpagemag.com/Articles/Read.aspx?GUID=54EB91DB-7577-47FB-AE56-DF0F0868D192 (accessed April 27, 2010).

15. Ibid.

16. Henry Abelove, Michele Aina Barale, and David M. Halperin, eds., *The Lesbian and Gay Studies Reader* (New York: Routledge Inc., 1993), 7.

17. Hiles, "Propagandizing Professors."

18. Michael Barone, "The Blame-America-First Crowd," RealClearPolitics.com, http://www.realclearpolitics.com/articles/2007/03/the_blameamericafirst_crowd.html (accessed April 27, 2010).

CHAPTER 27
When Manliness Is Outlawed, Only Outlaws Will Be Manly

1. Lisa Rein, "Down on the Ranch, President Wages War on the Underbrush," *Washington Post*, December 31, 2005, http://www.washingtonpost.com/wp-dyn/content/article/2005/12/30/AR2005123001326.html (accessed April 27, 2010).

2. Evgenia Peretz, "High Noon in Crawford," *Vanity Fair*, November 2005, http://www.vanityfair.com/politics/features/2005/11/crawford200511?currentPage=1 and http://www.vanityfair.com/politics/features/2005/11/crawford200511?currentPage=5 (accessed April 27, 2010).

3. Mark Simpson, "Here Come the Mirror Men," MarkSimpson.com, http://www.marksimpson.com/pages/journalism/mirror_men.html (accessed April 27, 2010).

4. *Oxford English Dictionary 2005*, s.v. "metrosexual."

5. Christina Hoff Sommers, *The War Against Boys: How Misguided Feminism Is Harming Our Young Men* (New York: Simon & Schuster, 2000), 14.

CHAPTER 28
SUMMARY (PART 3)

1. Associated Press, "Maine Middle School to Offer Birth Control," MSNBC.com, October 18, 2007, http://www.msnbc.msn.com/id/21358971 (accessed April 27, 2010).
2. Ibid.
3. West, *The Death of the Grown-Up: How America's Arrested Development Is Bringing Down Western Civilization*, 3.
4. C. S. Lewis, *Mere Christianity* (San Francisco: HarperSanFrancisco, 2001), 134.

CHAPTER 29: HEADSTANDS

1. Michael Barone, "The Blame-America-First Crowd," RealClearPolitics.com, March 19, 2007, http://www.realclearpolitics.com/articles/2007/03/the_blameamericafirst_crowd.html (accessed May 16, 2010).
2. Todd Gitlin, "Blaming America First," *Mother Jones* (January/February 2002) http://www.motherjones.com/commentary/columns/2002/01/blaming.html (accessed April 27, 2010).
3. Ted Goodman, ed., *The Forbes Book of Business Quotations* (New York: Black Dog and Leventhal Publishers, Inc., 1997), 14.
4. Stanley Kurtz, "Angry Talk," National Review Online, January 2, 2007, http://article.nationalreview.com/302063/angry-talk/stanley-kurtz (accessed May 16, 2010).

CHAPTER 30
HEADS UP

1. MSNBC suspended Shuster indefinitely in April 2010. Richard Huff, "MSNBC News Anchor David Shuster Canned for CNN Gig," *Daily News*, April 6, 2010, http://www.nydailynews.com/entertainment/tv/2010/04/06/2010-04-06_msnbcs_david_schuster_canned_from_msnbc_over_cnn_pilot.html (accessed April 27, 2010).
2. Kurtz, "Trading the Talk for the Walk?"
3. Steve Krakauer, "Bill Maher's Medical Meltdown Turns Off Guests, Confuses Audience," Mediaite.com, October 18, 2009, http://www.mediaite.com/tv/bill-mahers-medical-meltdown-turns-off-guests-confuses-audience/ (accessed May 16, 2010).
4. Robert Costa, "'They Just Want This Over,'" National Review Online, March 12, 2010, http://corner.nationalreview.com/post/q=MzU0MDYxMWEyOTdiNGU1OGU3ZjYzYmE3Y2ZlZDQ5NTY= (accessed April 27, 2010).
5. USA Patriotism!, as quoted from *Air Force Link*, November 3, 2004, http://www.usa-patriotism.com/stars/gsinise.htm (accessed April 27, 2010).
6. Ibid.
7. Gary Sinise and the Lt. Dan Band, http://www.ltdanband.com/ltdb_pages/links.html (accessed April 27, 2010).
8. Operational International Children, "Mission Statement," http://www.operation iraqichildren.org/ (accessed April 27, 2010).

9. Arnold R. Grahl, "Farrow Speaks Out on Polio, Darfur," Rotary International News, June 23, 2009, http://www.rotary.org/en/MediaAndNews/News/Pages/conv09june23_plenary3.aspx (accessed May 16, 2010).

10. A listing of editorials by Mia Farrow can be found on the Web site http://www.miafarrow.org by clicking on the editorials link.

11. Mike Nizza, "Mia Farrow's Darfur Gambit," The Lede blogs, New York Times, August 6, 2007, http://thelede.blogs.nytimes.com/2007/08/06/mia-farrows-darfur-gambit/ (accessed May 16, 2010).

12. Mia Farrow, "My Hunger Strike for Darfur," Huffington Post, April 19, 2009, http://www.huffingtonpost.com/mia-farrow/my-hunger-strike-for-darf_b_188741.html (accessed May 16, 2010).

13. Salem-News.com, "Actress Mia Farrow Joins Fast to Fight Hunger and Violence in Darfur," June 3, 2009, http://www.salem-news.com/articles/june032009/fast_darfur_6-3-09.php (accessed May 16, 2010).

14. Associated Press, "Spielberg Bails on Beijing Olympics Role," CBSNews.com, February 13, 2008, http://www.cbsnews.com/stories/2008/02/13/entertainment/main3827392.shtml (accessed May 16, 2010).

15. Associated Press, "Farrow Going to Darfur for China Protest," USAToday.com, April 4, 2008, http://www.usatoday.com/life/movies/2008-04-03-942892179_x.htm (accessed May 16, 2010).

16. As We Forgive, DVD, directed by Laura Waters Hinson (2009, n.p.: Team Marketing).

17. Refugees International, "Release: RI to Honor Mia Farrow and Ronan Farrow at 29th Anniversary Dinner," press release, April 28, 2008, http://www.refugeesinternational.org/press-room/press-release/release-ri-honor-mia-farrow-and-ronan-farrow-29th-anniversary-dinner (accessed May 16, 2010).

18. Christopher Hitchens, "Taking Sides," The Nation, September 26, 2002, http://www.thenation.com/doc/20021014/hitchens (accessed April 27, 2010).

19. Brent Baker, "Hitchens Gives the Finger to Maher's Audience for 'Frivolous' Jeering of Bush," NewsBusters, August 26, 2006, http://newsbusters.org/node/7190 (accessed April 27, 2010).

20. Ibid.

21. Ibid.

Conclusion
Righting a "Contrary" Culture

1. Newt Gingrich, "Everyone Agrees on a Lot of Things: Let's Do Them," originally published in the Des Moines Register, December 22, 2007, posted on Newt.org, http://www.newt.org/node/495 (accessed April 27, 2010).

2. Taylor Fife, "Initiative Targets Military Recruitment," Daily Californian, January 24, 2008, http://www.dailycal.org/article/100049/initiative_targets_military_recruitment (accessed April 27, 2010).

3. Ibid.

4. Ibid.

5. Penn & Teller, http://www.sho.com/site/ptbs/about.do (accessed April 28, 2010).

6. Sam Harris, *The End of Faith: Religion, Terror, and the Future of Reason* (New York: W.W. Norton & Co., 2004), 48.

7. Theodore Dalrymple, "What the New Atheists Don't See," *CityJournal*, Autumn 2007, http://www.city-journal.org/html/17_4_oh_to_be.html (accessed April 28, 2010).

8. Harris, *The End of Faith*, 52–53.